A New Bretton Woods
Rethinking International Economic Institutions and Arrangements

C. R. Neu

RAND Summer Institute

PREFACE

The first RAND Summer Institute was convened in July and August of 1992. Its overall purpose was threefold: to make conceptual progress on crucial American foreign and domestic policy issues, to help RAND plan future research, and to provide new ideas to the Administration that would be elected in November.

The institute comprised five week-long workshops that brought together nationally recognized experts from outside RAND and senior analysts from within. They addressed the following topics:

- Science, technology, and U.S. economic competitiveness;

- Peacekeeping and peacemaking after the Cold War;

- Reforming the U.S. health care system;

- Reshaping international economic institutions in the post-Cold War era;

- Alternative federal roles in precollegiate education.

The discussions have been summarized in publications prepared by the workshop leaders.

The RAND Summer Institute was supported by a major grant from Peter S. Bing. Supplemental funding was derived from RAND's endowment income.

FOREWORD

In August 1992, RAND convened a group of outside experts and RAND staff for a week-long workshop to discuss the possible need for reshaping international economic institutions and arrangements in light of changing economic and political circumstances. This workshop was one of five convened as part of the 1992 RAND Summer Institute.

To set the stage for the workshop, I prepared a short paper laying out an agenda for discussion and raising what seemed to me to be some key questions about the purposes and characteristics of international economic institutions and arrangements. As was to be expected with a group so experienced and well informed, workshop discussions ranged well beyond the questions I had originally posed. The workshop had little formal structure. No papers were presented. The entire week was given over to discussion and debate on the nature of the modern international economy and the institutions and mechanisms required to manage it. Frequently, these debates became quite intense, as opposing views were energetically and cogently argued. A wealth of expertise, insight, informed opinion, and thoughtful speculation was shared during the course of the week.

This report represents my attempt to capture the substance of the week's discussions. I have attempted to report accurately and without taking sides the topics debated, the positions taken, and the arguments advanced. My aims have been to note areas of general agreement and to explain the roots of disagreements that appeared in the course of our discussions. As the reader will see, we did not lack for differences of opinion. Among the participants in the workshop were forceful and articulate proponents of the major strands of current thinking about the nature and the roles of international economic institutions. Consequently, this summary of workshop discussions is also, I believe, a fair summary of the current academic and policy debate over these matters.

In accordance with the ground rules established in advance of the workshop, positions reported here are not attributed to particular participants. Neither have I made any attempt to document the sources of many views, empirical findings, or opinions referred to. In part, this reflects my desire to produce a timely summary of our discussions. It also reflects the fact that I simply do not know the sources of all of the referenced material. Free-ranging discussion with a group as broadly experienced as ours generates an enormous number of references to other studies, articles, and presentations. It is the nature of informal discussion not to be footnoted, however, and consequently my attempt to capture the content of this discussion is mostly without source citations as well. I apologize if it seems that I am appropriating other people's ideas for my own purposes. Any unclarity of presentation or of thought in this document should be attributed entirely to my failures as a reporter or interpreter of workshop discussions. Without exception, the arguments of the participants were clear and to the point.

A list of workshop attendees is provided in the appendix.

CONTENTS

In 1944, an international conference was convened in Bretton Woods, New Hampshire, to plan the structure of the postwar international economic environment. The economic institutions and arrangements that grew out of this conference—the International Monetary Fund (IMF), the International Bank for Reconstruction and Development (IBRD or, more commonly, the World Bank), and the General Agreement on Tariffs and Trade (GATT)—have shaped international economic relations for the past 45 years.

For the most part, these institutions and arrangements have served us well. But both the nature and the scale of international economic activity have changed enormously in 45 years, and it would be surprising if institutions and arrangements first designed in 1944 were still adequate to the task of managing today's international economy. The Bretton Woods institutions have changed, of course, with the times. Much of this change has been ad hoc in nature, though, and uncoordinated. What was once a more or less coherent set of institutions and arrangements for managing the world economy has begun to show gaps, redundancies, and misalignments. Interest is growing in a comprehensive rethinking of the structure and the rules of international economic relations, and of the roles of specific international institutions in managing these relations.

The original Bretton Woods conferees recognized the need for international cooperation and concerted action to achieve three primary ends: to create a system of exchange rates and international payments that would facilitate international trade and investment; to establish a set of rules to govern international trading relations; and

to provide the international credit necessary to support national efforts at economic reconstruction and development. Today, we might
add to these tasks a fourth: the effective regulation of economic
activity that is increasingly beyond the reach of purely national authorities. The notion is widely accepted that a smoothly functioning
international economic environment is an "international public
good"—an end that cannot be achieved solely through unilateral
actions by individual nations—and the need for some degree of international cooperation is not disputed. There is considerable controversy, however, over the nature and the specific objectives of this
cooperation and over the international institutions required to
manage it.

EXCHANGE RATES, INTERNATIONAL PAYMENTS, AND MACROECONOMIC COORDINATION

In 1973, the worldwide system of fixed exchange rates that had grown
out of the Bretton Woods conference collapsed. With it collapsed
any consensus on whether and how exchange rates should be managed. In the years since 1973, many smaller countries have continued to fix the value of their currency in relation to one or a group of
major currencies. Some larger industrialized countries have sought,
with varying degrees of success, to maintain stable exchange rates
among their currencies. (The Exchange Rate Mechanism of the European Community is the most prominent of such efforts.) The
world's major currencies, however—the dollar, the yen, and the
deutsche mark—have floated more or less freely against each other,
with exchange rates among them determined primarily by market
forces. This mixed exchange-rate regime has not performed in the
way that some analysts had expected, and the longstanding debate
over the relative merits of fixed and floating exchange-rate regimes
has been renewed.

The principal argument in favor of fixed exchange rates is that the
large swings in nominal and real exchange rates that have marked
the last 20 years threaten the continued viability of a liberal trading
regime. Large exchange-rate movements can undermine the international competitiveness of entire industries, forcing large-scale lay-
offs and laying idle capital equipment that may have many years of
functional life yet to run. In the face of such swings, national gov-

ernments will feel strong pressure to adopt protectionist measures. These pressures will be all the greater because there is always the possibility that exchange-rate movements will be reversed in a few years' time. Threatened industries may once again become competitive, if only they can be protected for a few years until exchange rates return to "normal." Proponents of fixed exchange rates believe that it is no coincidence that regional free-trade areas have been gaining in appeal since the collapse of the fixed-exchange-rate system. Within these free-trade zones, exchange rates are often relatively stable, and trade within a zone of currency stability does not carry the risks of exchange-rate-induced loss that are inherent in worldwide trade. Exchange-rate risk may also discourage long-term investment; why embark on a five-year effort to build a new plant when its viability could be wiped out by an exchange-rate movement? Finally, the requirement to maintain established exchange rates may force national monetary authorities to adopt a welcome policy discipline. Inflationary or destabilizing policies have international consequences, and a set of international rules that makes such policies less likely may be a valuable public good.

But what one observer sees as volatility, another sees as flexibility. Opponents of fixed exchange rates argue that the world is an uncertain place, and that national economies will continually be buffeted by "real-side" economic shocks—unexpected changes in the supply of or the demand for real goods and services. In the face of such shocks, real exchange rates *should* change. Flexible exchange rates provide a kind of shock-absorbing mechanism through which real-side shocks can be spread over many countries, lessening their impact on any one country. As a practical matter, in the face of such shocks, few countries will find it in their interest to adhere to international agreements to maintain fixed exchange rates—as the recent collapse of the European Exchange Rate Mechanism once again demonstrates. To these observers, efforts to fix exchange rates treat only a symptom of international economic instability, not its primary cause: ill-conceived government policies. Rather than fixing exchange rates, they argue, cooperative efforts should focus on encouraging nations to adopt policies that will lead to noninflationary, long-run growth. If such policies are instituted, exchange rates will take care of themselves.

INTERNATIONAL TRADE AND INVESTMENT

The international trading structure first laid out at the Bretton Woods conference and later codified in the General Agreement on Tariffs and Trade (GATT) is based on multilateralism and nondiscrimination. Trade concessions are to be negotiated in a multilateral setting, and concessions granted to one country are generally to be granted to all countries acceding to the GATT. In recent years, however, questions have been raised about the continued viability of this approach to setting trade rules. As trade policy differences have become more complex, the multilateral negotiating structure of GATT has become increasingly unwieldy. The current round of GATT negotiations has been effectively stalled for more than three years. As an alternative to waiting for worldwide reductions in trade barriers negotiated through the GATT, interest has been growing in preferential trading arrangements among smaller groups of countries. The most prominent of these arrangements have a regional character: the single European market and the North American free trade agreement. Others, not always regional in nature, have been proposed.

Few observers doubt the importance of concluding the current round of GATT negotiations. GATT is and will remain the best basis for worldwide trade. There is sharp division, though, about the wisdom of pursuing preferential trade arrangements in parallel with the GATT. Proponents of such arrangements see them as a way to achieve global trade liberalization in a piecemeal fashion. Like-minded countries can agree to reduce trade barriers among themselves, extending these concessions to additional countries as they agree to accept the rules of the group. As more and more countries join in these preferential trading arrangements, the goal of freer global trade will be approached.

Opponents of preferential trading arrangements consider these hopes naive and dangerous. Rather than providing an indirect route to more liberal world trade, they argue, the creation of preferential trading blocs will provide excuses and mechanisms for erecting yet higher barriers to trade between blocs.

ACCESS TO INTERNATIONAL CREDIT

At the time of the original Bretton Woods conference, private international capital and credit markets were only poorly developed and inadequate to the task of financing large-scale reconstruction or development programs. Moreover, private international capital flows were at that time seen as potentially destabilizing, and many observers of the day preferred to minimize reliance on private sources of international credit. For both of these reasons, the conferees agreed to the establishment of a multilateral development bank, the World Bank. Backed by national governments and managed by international civil servants, this bank was to channel credit to reconstruction and development efforts. In the years that followed, a number of regional development banks were also created.

Today, private international capital and credit markets are well developed and can provide credit to developing countries in amounts far larger than can be had through official channels. Also, the distrust of private international capital flows has largely dissipated (or at least been rendered irrelevant by the current huge volume of such flows). There is today some question about whether there is any longer a need for official multilateral sources of international credit.

Opponents of official international lending argue that official lenders are not necessarily better positioned than private lenders to recognize promising development programs, and that the willingness of official institutions to lend sometimes allows countries to postpone needed economic reforms. The discipline of the private market, they suggest, would force a more rapid adoption of necessary reforms and hence more rapid economic development. These opponents recognize that even today all countries do not have access to private international credit markets. They argue, however, that countries are denied access principally because they are viewed (usually correctly) as poor credit risks. Official assistance to such countries is desirable, and there are advantages to providing it through multilateral channels. But this assistance should properly come in the form of grants rather than loans. Making loans to countries that are not creditworthy is at best dishonest (because there is little likelihood that the loans will be repaid) and at worst counterproductive (because debtor countries may in fact try to repay them).

Proponents of official credit argue that private lenders frequently display herd-like behavior, all being much too ready to lend at some times and much too reluctant at others. This kind of behavior leads to overborrowing followed by severe credit droughts, such as we saw during the 1980s. Official institutions with substantial resources can provide liquidity during these credit droughts, thereby stabilizing both development programs and the international financial structure.

Besides providing credit, the international economic institutions, and particularly the IMF, have become arbiters of what constitutes acceptable economic policy for developing countries. Private lenders are frequently reluctant to extend credit to countries whose policies have not first been vetted by the IMF. Some observers find this a useful role for the IMF; borrowing countries cannot escape market discipline by playing one private lender off against another. Others, however, are uncomfortable with the dominance the IMF has gained in this regard. They note that there is no monopoly on wisdom about the nature of successful economic reform or development programs, and that there is no reason to believe IMF prescriptions will be optimal in all cases. They would prefer to see the IMF play a less central role in determining reform and development strategies.

INTERNATIONAL REGULATION

Recent years have seen a rapid internationalization of economic activities. Firms now straddle international boundaries, fully integrating operations located in multiple countries. Production, information, finance, and people have become increasingly mobile. As a consequence, national authorities are no longer able effectively to regulate some kinds of international business.

This is not altogether a bad thing. Governments are sometimes tempted to overregulate, and the ability of firms to move activities to other countries serves to check more extreme national regulatory tendencies. But in some industries (banking is a currently painful example), the need for at least some regulation is widely accepted. In such cases, some degree of international regulatory cooperation may be required.

Although there is general agreement on a number of basic principles regarding when and how to seek international regulatory cooperation, there remain intense disagreements about how to apply these principles in particular cases. Among the more controversial proposals for international cooperation are: cooperation among national tax authorities to guarantee the taxation of overseas investment income; efforts to control the trade in arms and "dual-use" technology; and general efforts to "harmonize" national regulatory regimes.

A NEW BRETTON WOODS

Policy choices of the sort summarized here cannot be resolved unilaterally by individual nations. The task of structuring the international economic environment is necessarily a collective undertaking. No nation is in a position today to dictate this new structure to the rest of the world or, through its forbearance, to make a structure work despite deviations by other nations from agreed-upon policies. What seems to be needed, then, is a new international consensus on how the international economy will function—figuratively, if not literally, a new Bretton Woods conference.

ACKNOWLEDGMENTS

The real authors of this report were the outside experts and RAND staff members who participated in the RAND Summer Institute workshop on International Economics from August 3 through August 7, 1992. (A list of workshop participants is provided in the appendix.) Their wisdom, experience, and insight provided the basis for this document. I am particularly grateful to my RAND colleagues Abraham S. Becker and Albert P. Williams, who helped me chair the workshop and offered helpful comments on earlier drafts of this report. Two RAND Graduate School fellows, Peter Cannon and Brent Boultinghouse, served as rapporteurs during the workshop. In writing this report, I depended heavily on their summaries of workshop discussions. Laura Zakaras offered counsel on presentational matters. All of the above did their best to keep my thinking clear and correct. Any deficiencies that remain despite their efforts are due solely to my failings.

Chapter One

INTRODUCTION

As World War II was coming to an end, representatives of the soon-to-be victorious Allied nations gathered in Bretton Woods, New Hampshire, to plan the structure of the postwar international economic environment. Earlier arrangements for international trade and payments had collapsed disastrously during the 1930s, and the conferees sought to devise a set of institutions and arrangements for the future that would prove more robust. The conferees also recognized that the end of hostilities would present the world with a reconstruction task of unprecedented magnitude. All nations had a stake in the success of this reconstruction, and means had to be found for channeling global resources into the reconstruction effort.

The institutions and arrangements that grew out of the 1944 Bretton Woods conference—the International Monetary Fund (IMF), the International Bank for Reconstruction and Development (IBRD or World Bank), and, less directly, the General Agreement on Tariffs and Trade (GATT)—have served as the principal pillars of the international economic environment for the past 45 years. Although there is considerable debate about whether different institutions or different policies pursued by the same institutions might have served the international economy better, the international economic environment that was given rough shape at Bretton Woods has proved largely successful. In most of the world (or at least in most of the world that participated in the Bretton Woods institutions), overall economic activity has expanded and material welfare has improved at rates that are high by almost any historical standard. International trade and investment have expanded even more rapidly than general economic activity. The countries most devastated by the war were

1

rebuilt, and development assistance has been extended to many other countries. Most important, the world has avoided economic catastrophes like the Great Depression.

But the Bretton Woods institutions were very much the products of their time. They were designed to deal with the international economic problems that had beset the world in the then-recent past and that could be envisioned in the near future. The operating styles and policies of these institutions were established in the early years of the Cold War and reflected the mindset, the political circumstances, and the relative economic standing of nations as they were in the 1950s and 1960s.

The world, of course, has changed since then. The scale and nature of international economic activity have changed enormously since 1944, and so have the kinds of problems that require coordinated or cooperative efforts among nations. Years of sometimes harsh experience have forced revised thinking about economic policy and paths to successful economic development. Most dramatically, political realities and relative economic rankings have changed. Once dominant in every aspect of international relations, the United States is now—in economic terms at least—only the first among a number of more or less equals. It would be surprising if the set of institutions and arrangements, no matter how well designed, that was right for the world of 1944 were right for the world of today.

To be sure, the Bretton Woods institutions have changed over the years in response to changes in the international economic environment. New institutions and arrangements have been created to handle new problems (for example, the Organization for Economic Cooperation and Development, the European Community, and the G-7 consultative process). Old institutions (the Bank for International Settlements, for example) have taken on important new roles. These changes, though, have been largely ad hoc in nature, and not always coordinated among institutions. What was once a more or less consistent set of institutions and arrangements for managing the most important aspects of international economic relations has begun to show gaps, redundancies, and misalignments. Distinctions between institutions have become blurred. Arguably important functions are not being performed by any institution. Some institutions have taken on tasks for which they may not be well suited, by reason of their structures, memberships, or traditions. Unable to achieve desired ends through established multilateral mechanisms, nations are increasingly resorting to unilateral or bilateral actions, sometimes to the detriment of other nations. The system of international economic institutions and arrangements devised at Bretton Woods is beginning to show its age, and there is a growing perception that the time has come for a comprehensive rethinking of how we manage the international economy.[1]

This rethinking needs to be comprehensive because no aspect of the international economy is entirely independent. How we choose to manage exchange rates, for example, may have implications for how we set rules for international trade and investment. Policies and regulations affecting international capital flows will have much to do with the kind of arrangements we make to foster economic reconstruction and development. If we are going to think seriously about how to reshape a part of the international economic structure, we have to think about the entire structure.

The times are conducive to rethinking the international economic structure. The end of the Cold War and the collapse of the Soviet bloc have provided an impetus for a general reconsideration of all international relations—political, military, and economic. We are at a crossroads not entirely unlike the one perceived by the Bretton Woods conferees. Confronted with a new world, we have a chance to shape a new system of international economic institutions as a part of a new system of general international relations—as a part of a "new world order." More ominously, the end of World War II presented the Bretton Woods conferees with the real prospect of political and social turmoil if the reconstruction effort should fail. The collapse of communism confronts the current generation of policymakers with a similar specter. The times, then, present both an opportunity and an urgent need to consider the adequacy of existing international economic institutions and arrangements.

---

[1]The Mount Washington Hotel, where the Bretton Woods conferees met in 1944, was auctioned by federal banking regulators in June 1991. The hotel had been seized by the Federal Deposit Insurance Corporation when its owner, the Eliot Savings Bank of Boston, failed, a victim of changing financial circumstances.

The basic problem that the Bretton Woods conferees faced, and which we still face today, is that a smoothly operating international economic system—one that facilitates international trade and investment, provides adequate stability and predictability to allow long-term planning, and is conducive to economic growth and development—is a true "public good." No single nation is able to establish or to maintain such a system through unilateral action. Some degree of international cooperation, coordination, or harmonization is required. This concerted international action can range from simple agreement on "rules of the game" to the creation of activist, supranational institutions.

There is little debate over the "public good" character of most aspects of international economic relations. Almost all observers agree on the need for a common international understanding on how trade, payments, development finance, and so on are to be managed. There is great controversy, however, over the specifics of this understanding—the exact goals of joint action, the best means for achieving these goals, when common "rules of the game" will be sufficient, and when direct action is required—and over what international institutions are required to specify, interpret, enforce, or implement this understanding. Thoughtful observers propose and argue cogently for very different approaches. In some cases, differences arise from disputes about facts. These disputes can be resolved, in theory at least, through empirical research. More often, differing views about appropriate policies spring from differing beliefs about such fundamental matters as the capabilities and proper roles of government, the natural tendencies of national policymakers, and the course of future political developments. Only time and experience will resolve these differences.

This report seeks to summarize the debates over how to structure various aspects of international economic relations. Without taking sides, I try to present the arguments for maintaining existing institutions and arrangements, the principal proposals for changing them, and the thinking that underlies each position. As much as possible, I try to characterize the fundamental differences in outlook that give rise to different policy prescriptions.

For the sake of organizational convenience, the remainder of this report is divided into five sections. The first four of these deal, respectively, with macroeconomic coordination and exchange-rate stabilization, international trade and investment, provisions for channeling capital and technical assistance to developing and transforming economies, and international harmonization of regulatory practices. Although convenient, these divisions are somewhat artificial, and it will become apparent that none of these topics can be discussed without some references to the others. A final section offers a summary of the major policy choices we will face in the next few years and some comments about the basic differences in outlook that lead to different policy prescriptions with regard to each of these choices.

Chapter Two

EXCHANGE RATES, INTERNATIONAL PAYMENTS, AND MACROECONOMIC COORDINATION

In 1944, the thinking about a system for international payments was dominated by the requirements of international trade. Vivid in the memories of the Bretton Woods conferees were the competitive devaluations of the 1930s, which had contributed to the collapse of international trade. Also of concern was the need for some source of international liquidity to support the rebirth of international trade in the postwar world. With most of the world's major economies in ruins, few currencies were convertible. Without a widely accepted "international money" in which accounts could be settled, trade could hardly flourish.

THE BRETTON WOODS SOLUTION

The solution to these problems devised at Bretton Woods was the creation of a system of fixed exchange rates in which the values of all other currencies were specified relative to the dollar. Currencies were to be devalued only after international consultations and never in pursuit of "beggar thy neighbor" policies. Stocks of international liquidity—initially, only gold and dollars were acceptable as international currencies—were pooled to form the International Monetary Fund (IMF). A nation in temporary need of liquidity to maintain a fixed exchange rate could borrow dollars from the IMF. Because only a few nations were likely to need liquidity at any given time, the pooling of reserves was an ingenious device to make the limited stocks of international currencies stretch further. These arrangements also gave nations some say in the formulation of each other's

7

macroeconomic policies. A nation wishing to devalue its currency first had to obtain confirmation from the IMF that a "fundamental imbalance" in its international payments existed and necessitated a devaluation. A nation seeking credit from the IMF to support an exchange rate had to submit to economic policy conditions that became more stringent as the size of its borrowings grew. So that it could recognize "fundamental imbalances" and set conditions appropriate for eliminating liquidity problems, the IMF was set up with a sizable analytic staff.[1]

With attention fixed on the need to create an environment conducive to international trade, the articles of agreement of the IMF specified that member nations would take no actions to restrict international payments arising from current account transactions. Restrictions on capital account transactions, however, were permitted and in some cases encouraged by IMF conditionality. In this, the IMF articles of agreement reflected the then-prevailing suspicion of international movements of private capital. Both balance-of-payments accounting and policy thinking of the day distinguished between flows of "long-term" capital—flows associated with direct foreign investment and the purchase of long-maturity bonds—and flows of "short-term" capital—typically movements of funds into and out of demand deposits and other short-maturity instruments. Long-term capital flows were generally viewed as productive and benign. Short-term capital flows, though, were seen as having little economic value and as potentially destabilizing. As the experience of the 1930s had demonstrated, changes in fickle market sentiment could trigger large flows of "hot money" that would undermine efforts to maintain stable exchange rates. Measures to inhibit such flows were widely seen as justified and even prudent. A nation facing an international

---

[1]Despite the ingenuity of the IMF design, the international payment arrangements established at Bretton Woods proved inadequate to the task of restoring intra-European trade and the convertibility of European currencies in the immediate aftermath of World War II. Only the creation in 1950 of a European Payments Union as a part of the Marshall Plan allowed the resumption of trade among the European countries. In essence, this payments union provided a mechanism for netting credits and debits in each European currency. Settling the remaining balances (necessarily in dollars, because European currencies remained nonconvertible) required many fewer then-scarce dollars than would have been necessary to settle transactions individually.

liquidity problem, then, was not to impede international trade by restricting payments for imports. It could, however, impose capital controls.

The Bretton Woods exchange-rate system was asymmetric in the economic policy obligations that it imposed on participating countries. Only those countries facing liquidity shortages had a need to borrow from the Fund, and consequently Fund conditionality operated always to encourage contractionary macroeconomic policies. Countries with surpluses of foreign exchange had no need of the Fund's resources, and consequently no opportunity arose for the Fund to encourage more expansionary policies. As matters developed (and contrary to the original intent of the Bretton Woods conferees), the United States enjoyed a special position in the Bretton Woods exchange-rate arrangement. Other countries were required to maintain exchange rates fixed against the dollar. Typically, this meant that they were required to intervene as necessary in foreign exchange markets, buying or selling their currencies to maintain exchange rates vis-à-vis the dollar within narrow bands. When intervention alone was insufficient to maintain the desired exchange rate, changes in domestic monetary or fiscal policies were to be undertaken. The United States had no such obligations. It was required merely to stand ready to convert dollars into gold at a fixed rate. The result of this was a crude sort of international macroeconomic policy coordination (also unintended by the Bretton Woods conferees): Other countries were required to adjust their policies in response to U.S. policies.

THE COLLAPSE OF THE BRETTON WOODS MECHANISM

The fixed-exchange-rate system devised at Bretton Woods collapsed in 1971, primarily because other industrialized nations would no longer accept U.S. dictation of global macroeconomic policies. Unwilling to tolerate the rates of monetary expansion (and the inflation they feared such expansion would bring) necessary to maintain fixed exchange rates vis-à-vis the dollar, these countries went their own macroeconomic way. Without an obligation to maintain fixed exchange rates, countries no longer bore a responsibility to coordinate macroeconomic policies. And without coordinated macroeconomic policies, no set of fixed exchange rates could be sustained.[2]

The fixed-exchange-rate system was temporarily patched up with the so-called Smithsonian agreement,[3] but it soon collapsed again, for basically the same reason. Since 1973, the world's major currencies—dollar, yen, and deutsche mark (or, more recently, the ECU)—have floated against each other. Most of the world's other currencies are fixed to one or another of these major currencies or to some basket of currencies, and it is probably most accurate to think of the current situation as typified by a small number of large currency blocs. Within each bloc, exchange rates are managed with greater or lesser degrees of formality and remain relatively fixed. Across blocs, though, we see both day-to-day volatility and large longer-term swings in both nominal and real exchange rates.

The shift from the fixed-exchange-rate system to one in which the major currencies floated against each other did not reflect a conscious policy choice.[4] It happened because it was impossible any longer to maintain fixed exchange rates. But there had been considerable prior debate over the wisdom of continued adherence to the Bretton Woods system. Proponents of floating exchange rates argued that floating rates would give national policymakers an additional degree of freedom in formulating national economic policies. In the pursuit of national objectives, for example, these policymakers could choose national inflation rates higher or lower than those of

---

[2]This situation has been wryly characterized by the *Financial Times* as follows: "Coordination used to mean that the U.S. did what it wanted, while everybody else did what the U.S. wanted. Now, it means that the major players first argue with one another, whereupon each does precisely what it wants." Quoted in *Changing Our Ways: America and the New World,* Carnegie Endowment for International Peace, 1992.

[3]The Bretton Woods system collapsed in May 1971, when West Germany allowed the mark to float. In December 1971, meetings at the Smithsonian Institution in Washington resulted in agreement essentially to reestablish the Bretton Woods exchange-rate regime, but at realigned parities and without any requirement that the United States convert dollars into gold. This final attempt at global exchange-rate stability collapsed in March 1973.

[4]In 1976, almost three years after the fact, the IMF Articles of Agreement were formally amended to allow floating exchange rates. Member nations were urged, however, to avoid "manipulating exchange rates . . . to gain an unfair competitive advantage over other members."

other nations.   Over time, it was argued, nominal exchange rates would adjust smoothly to reflect differential inflation rates.

Further, because foreign exchange markets respond more rapidly to changes in money supply than do domestic goods and labor markets, adjustments in money-supply growth rates would yield changes in exchange rates that were not fully matched—at least in the short run—by changes in domestic prices and wages.   Thus, countries faced with demand or supply shocks could, by changes in monetary policy, allow the foreign sector of the economy to bear some of the burden of adjustment.   A country in recession, for example, could expand its domestic money supply, depressing the value of its currency and, temporarily, stimulating foreign demand for domestically produced goods.

The automatic and continuous adjustment of floating exchange rates would also eliminate both the need for occasional large exchange-rate realignments and the associated large flows of speculative capital that had characterized the fixed-exchange-rate system.   Relieved of the responsibility to defend specific exchange rates, national authorities could dispense with the arsenal of capital controls, payments restrictions, multiple exchange rates, and controlled interest rates that they had used to counter market forces that pushed exchange rates away from established parities.   Such restrictions on the operation of market forces inevitably introduce distortions into national and international economies, and overall welfare would be increased by their removal.

Finally, currency-market speculators who persisted in selling a currency when it was below its equilibrium value or buying it when it was above its equilibrium value would lose money over the long term.   Thus, speculators whose actions served to destabilize foreign-exchange markets would eventually be driven from the market.   Only those speculators who somehow managed to stabilize exchange rates by moving them more quickly toward their equilibrium values would be left.

But the theoretical promise of floating exchange rates has not been realized.   Day-to-day, week-to-week, and month-to-month volatility of nominal exchange rates has been much higher than most proponents of floating rates had expected.   Real exchange rates have shown very large swings that have persisted for years at a time, only to be subsequently reversed. The real value of the dollar, for example, rose 72 percent against the yen from late 1978 to early 1985 and then declined by 46 percent in a space of just three years, from early 1985 to early 1988. Exchange-rate swings of this magnitude can play havoc with investment plans and production decisions. A plan, for example, to build an automobile plant in the United States might make good business sense at today's exchange rate. But five years from now, when the plant is ready to begin production, a very different constellation of exchange rates might leave this plant without a hope of competing successfully in international markets. Faced with such uncertainty, it would not be surprising if investors were reluctant to commit to large investment projects in industries where a changing exchange rate might expose them to ruinous foreign competition.

Where investments have been made, large exchange-rate movements can wipe out the viability of entire industries. With one set of exchange rates, production in the United States of autos, steel, or computers might be quite viable. With another constellation of exchange rates, it might be impossible. When exchange rates move, potentially productive plants may be idled. Workers will have to be retrained and will perhaps have to move to new cities in order to find jobs in new industries. Communities favored by a swing in exchange rates will have to build new schools, roads, and sewers to accommodate a growing population, while still-functional schools, roads, and sewers may be abandoned in areas hard hit by exchange-rate changes. If a movement in exchange rates reflects a permanent change in the productivity of workers or industries in one nation relative to those of some other nation, then such adjustment costs are unavoidable. The best policy in these circumstances is usually just to get on with the necessary adjustments. This will be painful enough. But what if the exchange-rate change is reversed in a few years? The adjustment costs already borne may be effectively lost, as we rebuild or reopen the factories and towns we just closed. Alternatively, we might simply do without the factories and jobs already lost but which might have been perfectly viable had there been no exchange-rate swing in the first place. A final diabolical element is added by the fact that it can be impossible to know whether an exchange-rate movement is permanent or likely to be reversed in a couple of years. Thus, it is hard to know whether we should undertake painful but necessary adjustments or just hold on until exchange rates move back again.[5]

Not surprisingly, national governments have revealed a general preference for less exchange volatility. Of the 154 members of the IMF in 1991, only 27 pursued exchange-rate policies characterized by the Fund as "independently floating." Many smaller countries peg their currencies to one of the major currencies or to a basket of major currencies. Industrialized countries have created institutions to encourage stability. The most ambitious and—until recently, at least—successful of these has been the Exchange Rate Mechanism (ERM) of the European Community. But faced with the choice of matching high German interest rates in order to maintain the value of their currencies or cutting interest rates in the hopes of spurring economic growth, the United Kingdom and Italy opted out of the fixed-rate arrangement in September 1992. The political and economic costs of maintaining fixed exchange rates were just too high. It is too early to tell whether or in what form the ERM will survive. Less ambitious (in part because of the participants' reluctance to subscribe fully to the goals of exchange-rate stabilization and policy coordination) has been the somewhat sporadic G-7 consultative process, through which the major industrialized countries have occasionally sought to adjust macroeconomic policies to move exchange rates.

In today's international economic environment, exchange-rate stability—at least among the world's major currencies—will be possible only through close coordination of national macroeconomic policies. Direct currency-market intervention and restrictions on capital flows, the cornerstones of the Bretton Woods system, will no longer suffice. The growth of truly international financial markets and the proliferation of sophisticated financial instruments in the last 20 years has rendered effective control of capital movements among major financial centers impossible. Transactions worth tens of millions of dollars, yen, or marks can be concluded nearly instantaneously by wire in any of several international financial centers, some well beyond the reach (if necessary) of monetary authorities in

---

[5]This kind of policy dilemma can, of course, be created by events other than changes in real exchange rates. Oil-price increases in the 1970s and early 1980s, for example, set in motion painful adjustment processes that in many cases had to be undone when oil prices fell in the mid-1980s.

the countries issuing any of the currencies involved. The volume of capital that can flow quickly from country to country or from currency to currency today is huge, dwarfing the resources that national monetary authorities could plausibly deploy for currency-market intervention. If financial markets perceive even a small likelihood that inconsistent policies will bring a realignment of exchange rates, very large volumes can rapidly move through foreign-exchange markets as asset holders seek to position themselves on the correct side of the expected exchange-rate change. By trying to defend an untenable exchange rate, monetary authorities create situations (so-called one-way bets) in which speculation against a weak currency entails no risk. Thus the adage (correct in a floating-rate regime) that destabilizing speculators will lose is stood on its head, and instability is actually increased. In most cases, national authorities—or an international authority, for that matter—will be powerless to counter large speculative flows through direct intervention and can stand to lose billions in futile efforts to stem a speculative tide. Only by avoiding the policy inconsistency in the first place and by having a credible policy to remove quickly whatever inconsistencies may from time to time appear could the issuers of the major currencies preserve exchange-rate stability.

IS A RETURN TO FIXED EXCHANGE RATES DESIRABLE?

Neither the desire for more stability nor the mechanisms created so far to facilitate policy coordination have yet done much to stabilize exchange rates among the dollar, yen, and deutsche mark/ECU. No one argues that exchange-rate volatility is desirable. But what one observer sees as volatility, another sees as flexibility, and there is considerable debate over whether the potential gains arising from direct efforts to reduce uncertainty about exchanges rates are sufficient to justify the surrender of national policy autonomy necessary to achieve greater stability.

At its heart, this is a debate over which part of the international economy should be thought of as the cart and which part the horse. One camp favors setting explicit targets for exchange rates and adjusting national economic policies as necessary to maintain these rates. The other camp would prefer to see nations pursue increasingly similar goals in formulating their macroeconomic policies.

Such policies, this second camp argues, will eventually bring more stable exchange rates without the need for formal exchange-rate targets. Where one comes out on this issue hinges critically on one's beliefs about the principal problems that economic policymakers will face in the coming years.

THE ARGUMENT FOR FIXED EXCHANGE RATES

Proponents of a return to some system of fixed exchange rates argue that without a credible mechanism for stabilizing exchange rates, maintaining a liberal international trading regime will become increasingly difficult. The problem is that, in today's global markets, a substantial change in exchange rates can destroy the competitive viability of major national industries. (Consider, for example, the position of the U.S. auto industry when the dollar became very strong in the early 1980s.) Governments cannot easily remain indifferent to the fates of entire industries and may be hard pressed in such circumstances to resist calls for protectionist policies. Worse, because tariffs will provide little protection against the consequences of large exchange-rate swings, governments will be increasingly prone to adopt quantitative import restrictions—generally regarded as the worst of all possible trade restrictions—to protect domestic industries threatened by exchange-rate changes. Proponents of this view argue that it is no accident that we are seeing an increased reliance on quantitative trade restrictions and managed trade arrangements since the collapse of the fixed-exchange-rate system.

Also, changing exchange rates can complicate comparisons of prices in domestic and foreign markets, opening the door to charges that producers in one country are "dumping" their products abroad at prices lower than they are charging in their home market. Proponents of fixed exchange rates are not surprised by the fact that dumping complaints and antidumping actions are becoming more common.

Neither are supporters of fixed rates surprised by the rise in interest in regional trading blocs and the (alleged) tendency of such trading blocs to raise barriers against imports from outside the bloc. Regional trading blocs, in their view, are roughly coincident with zones of exchange-rate stability. (Consider the European Community, the

North American free trade area, or a possible Asian free trade area composed of countries that link their currencies to the yen.) Trade within blocs will not be much affected by exchange-rate changes, but trade between blocs can be disrupted by exchange-rate swings. Governments seeking to minimize industrial dislocations may be tempted to insulate industries from exchange-rate-related uncertainties by restricting competition from outside the bloc.

Proponents of fixed exchange rates also argue that uncertainties about exchange rates several years in the future may discourage investment in industries that are subject to foreign competition. Wise investors, they argue, will prefer investment in production of nontradables, where exchange-rate changes will have little effect. A consequence of this behavior may be a bias toward investment in service industries and away from investment in manufacturing. With investment in new plant and equipment lagging, productivity growth in the manufacturing sector will show. While it is impossible confidently to attribute causality in these matters, and while many other factors are obviously at work, some observers have noted that the worldwide decline in rates of manufacturing productivity growth is at least roughly contemporaneous with the period of floating exchange rates.

More generally, proponents of fixed exchange rates point out that the periods of most rapid economic growth and most rapid expansion of world trade have coincided with periods in which a more or less formal system of fixed exchange rates prevailed: the era of the gold standard (1879–1913) and the era of the fixed-rate dollar standard (1945–1971). Both trade and growth collapsed disastrously, of course, during the interwar period, when exchange rates were very unstable, and the growth of both has slowed markedly since the end of the Bretton Woods exchange-rate system in 1971.

For proponents of fixed exchange rates, the most important objective of an exchange-rate regime is not to reduce or to eliminate day-to-day, week-to-week, or month-to-month volatility in exchange rates. Rather, it is to assure that real exchange rates remain more or less constant in the long run—over periods of years. In theory, short-term exchange-rate volatility can gum up the works of international financial markets, as participants in these markets demand premiums to compensate them for exchange-rate risk. These risk premiums add to the costs of each transaction and could, at the margin, discourage some otherwise beneficial transactions. But markets and instruments have been developed to provide low-cost opportunities for hedging foreign exchange risks on financial instruments with maturities up to a year or so. (For some kinds of instruments, longer-term hedging is possible.) Further, empirical efforts to identify risk premiums that are positively associated with the degree of exchange-rate volatility have generally failed, suggesting that the true costs of short-run exchange-rate volatility may be minor.

Long-term swings in real exchange rates can be more problematic. Investors in plant, equipment, or human capital have no generally effective ways to hedge the risks they face from the possibility of major exchange-rate changes several years in the future.[6] Consequently, we might expect some reluctance to make long-term investments in sectors where foreign competition is potentially important. Further, because those who have made such decisions in the past will necessarily be exposed to the consequences of exchange-rate changes, we might expect these investors to seek government protection aggressively when rates turn against them. These two problems can be avoided only if international cooperation offers both the prospect (to encourage investment) and the reality (to minimize pleas for protection) of real exchange rates that are stable over periods of years.

How attractive one finds the prospect of formally fixed exchange rates depends also on the kinds of shocks that one expects national policymakers to have to deal with. During the 1970s, 1980s, and per-

---

[6]In technical terms, the problem here is one of moral hazard. To put the matter simply, the owner of a factory can protect himself fully against future exchange-rate changes only if he is able to sell forward, at a price fixed today, his expected output some years in the future. Such forward contracts do not exist in most goods markets, however, principally because of the difficulty of insuring future production. (Problems arise, for example, because the insurer will not be able to distinguish between production shortfalls that are due to factors truly beyond the control of the factory owner and those that are the consequences of the owner's laziness, incompetence, or malfeasance.) Thus, the medium- and long-term exchange-rate risks faced by owners of productive capital can seldom be hedged. For a more complete discussion of this issue, see Ronald I. McKinnon and K. C. Fung, *Floating Exchange Rates and the New Interbloc Protectionism: Tariffs Versus Quotas*, Memorandum No. 302, The Center for Research in Economic Growth, Stanford University, February 1992.

haps even the early 1990s, the major shocks were from the real side of the economy: reductions in worldwide oil production, debt-servicing difficulties among developing countries, large tax cuts in the United States, significant changes in levels of public spending (especially for defense), and the cost of German reunification. More importantly, these shocks affected different economies to very different degrees. Japan, totally dependent on imported oil, suffered a much greater change in its terms of trade because of oil-price changes than did the United States. Japanese banks, however, had much less credit exposure to developing countries than did U.S. banks. Germany and, more generally, Europe are bearing the costs of German reunification. U.S. budget deficits of the 1980s and 1990s affected principally the United States. Even among the most ardent supporters of fixed exchange rates, few would argue that efforts to stabilize exchange rates during these turbulent times would have been feasible or desirable. In the face of developments like those we saw in the 1970s, 1980s, and early 1990s, real exchange rates *should* change. A system of fixed exchange rates would have robbed national policymakers of one degree of policy freedom as they tried to cope with shocks. In the end, these policymakers would have (and should have) bowed to the inevitable and changed exchange rates. (In 1992, faced with the economic consequences of German reunification, British and Italian authorities did precisely this.) Shocks of this magnitude that affect countries so differently will create just the sorts of "fundamental imbalances" that will require exchange-rate changes.

Strong supporters of fixed exchange rates see these kinds of shocks as unlikely in the future. The world's major economies have become so intertwined, they argue, that no economy will be able to escape the consequences of substantial shocks. With the end of the Cold War, major changes in military expenditure are unlikely. As economies become more closely linked, the domestic effects of fiscal policy changes will more quickly leak out through trade and capital movements to other economies. In the future, the shocks most likely to have differential effects on the major economies are those that arise from the monetary side of the economy: large changes in the demand for money because of changes in the way economic activities are carried out or erratic monetary policies by national authorities. But these are precisely the kinds of shocks that fixed exchange rates would help to minimize. Pressure on the exchange rate could serve as an early warning to central banks that their policies are out of line or that policy adjustments are required to compensate for changing money demand. In the future, proponents of fixed rates argue, the need for national policy autonomy will be reduced, and the discipline inherent in a system of fixed exchange rates may actually help to prevent the kinds of shocks that are most likely.

THE ARGUMENT AGAINST FIXED EXCHANGE RATES

Opponents of a formal system of fixed exchange rates find reasons to be skeptical about all of the above arguments. While they recognize the theoretical possibility that real exchange-rate instability could lead to increased pressure for protectionist policies, they question whether there is any real evidence that such policies are becoming more common or more restrictive. Japan, they argue, has opened its markets significantly in recent years (although there is still much room for further progress in this regard). Throughout the developing world, trade restrictions have also been reduced.[7] Increasing use of quantitative restrictions, they argue, is a consequence not of exchange-rate volatility but of the success of past rounds of multilateral trade negotiations, which have permanently bound tariffs at very low rates. Even the effects of changing real exchange rates on the fortunes of specific industries is far from established. Just as important in the modern environment may be cost advantages arising from economies of scale or exploitation of new technologies.

Most important, they argue, any supposition that the world will be immune to the kinds of real-side shocks that characterized the 1970s through the early 1990s is at best premature. The world is an unstable place in which national economies are continually buffeted by surprises and shocks: an oil-price change here, a crop failure there, a technological breakthrough, a war, or a flood of refugees. Shocks are shocking precisely because they are not anticipated, and the fact that it is difficult to forecast future disturbances of the sort we have seen in the last 20 years may suggest nothing more than the notion that

---

[7]Proponents of fixed rates counter this observation by pointing out that most developing countries in fact maintain exchange rates fixed against the currencies of their principal trading partners.

we are likely to be surprised in the future. Nations and national economies are and will remain different, and it would be surprising indeed if they were not affected differently by unforeseen developments.

Trying to control exchange rates in such a world is probably infeasible and possibly undesirable. In the face of real-side shocks that affect countries differentially, policymakers should be free to allow changing real exchange rates to spread some of the burden of adjustment to the foreign sector. Because real wages adjust only slowly to economic shocks, keeping the real exchange rate fixed forces the full burden of adjustment onto the domestic goods and labor markets.[8] An exchange-rate system that allows shocks affecting one country to be spread, through real exchange-rate changes, to other countries might be a valuable public good. Since nations can have no prior assurance that they will be immune to shocks, they might find it desirable to subscribe to an exchange-rate system that allows these unexpected burdens to be shared. Perhaps more to the point, when movements in the real exchange rate offer some prospect of easing domestic adjustment burdens, sovereign nations will be tempted to allow exchange rates to move, even if they have previously agreed to keep them fixed. If nations adhere to agreements to maintain fixed exchange rates and if there are lags in adjusting rates (as inevitably there will be), efforts to promote exchange-rate stability may serve to delay adjustment to permanent changes in international supply and demand conditions. If markets perceive the need for exchange realignments before authorities get around to making the required realignments, "one-way bets" will be created, and given the ease today with which capital can flow from one currency to another, exchange rates may actually be made less stable than they would have been without a mechanism to peg exchange rates. The announced policy of sticking to what foreign exchange markets saw as a clearly untenable sterling/deutsche mark exchange rate in September 1992 almost certainly encouraged a run on sterling, creating

---

[8]An interesting thought experiment is to consider what the consequences might have been for Texas, Oklahoma, and other parts of the U.S. oil patch if, in the face of sharply declining oil prices in the mid-1980s, these states had been able to devalue their currencies vis-à-vis those of other states. By lowering the costs of labor in the oil patch, such a devaluation would, presumably, have spread some of the job losses experienced there to other parts of the United States.

much more turmoil in European financial markets than would have been seen if sterling had been floating freely.

This is not to say that the current situation is the best that one might hope for. Noninflationary economic growth is in important respects a public good: If one nation manages it, others will have an easier time doing the same. Thus, each nation has an interest in the success of others, and there is reason for devising international arrangements that allow nations to encourage and support each other in the pursuit of these goals. But to seek formally fixed exchange rates is to treat a symptom—and only one symptom at that—rather than the underlying disease. The real problems, in the view of opponents of fixed exchange rates, are unpredictable real-side shocks that affect economies differentially, and the variations in national economic policies—wise or otherwise—that nations adopt in response to these shocks. No mechanism to fix exchange rates will eliminate shocks and price stickiness, and there is no guarantee that a fixed-exchange-rate regime will encourage wiser national policy choices.

Rather than seeking to coordinate specific macroeconomic policies to achieve a single end—exchange-rate stability—opponents of formally pegged exchange rates suggest that a more fruitful strategy would be for nations to agree on common approaches to policy formation and let specific outcomes, like exchange rates, take care of themselves. Specifically, these analysts suggest that national policymakers commit themselves not to the maintenance of exchange-rate stability but to the maintenance of domestic price stability. This, they argue, would do more to encourage investment—in both the traded- and nontraded-goods sectors—than would a commitment to exchange-rate stability.   Indeed, if all countries truly adhered to policies of promoting price stability, inflation rates would gradually decline and converge, interest rates would stabilize, and exchange rates would, automatically, stabilize.[9] When fundamental international supply and demand conditions change, nominal and real ex-

---

[9]One reason that a regime of floating exchange rates did not live up to its advance billing, some argue, is that the advance billing did not adequately take into account the consequences of shifting market expectations about future inflation rates in different countries. Because higher inflation rates are typically more uncertain inflation rates, failure by a number of nations to control inflation during the 1970s and 1980s led to uncertainty about future inflation rates, frequent changes in expectations about future inflation, and volatile exchange rates.

change rates would change as well. These changes, though, would be justified and proper. Any system that tried to prevent them would be doing more harm than good.

Even without fixed exchange rates and specifically coordinated macroeconomic policies, though, there would still be a need for some form of international macroeconomic cooperation. In the modern world, even the best efforts to maintain domestic price stability will be at least partially undermined by changes in real exchange rates with respect to the currencies of major trading partners. Some kind of international forum, then, in which nations reviewed at least the general outlines of each other's policies might be useful.

WHAT INSTITUTION?

Both proponents and opponents of formally fixed exchange rates would agree that some international institution, arrangement, or forum for fostering international macroeconomic coordination or cooperation would be useful. They disagree on the nature, the extent, the specificity, and the targets of this coordination or cooperation, but there is consensus that there really is an international public good here that cannot be obtained solely through unilateral national actions.

In the original Bretton Woods scheme, the IMF was the institution that was supposed to facilitate the necessary cooperation. As we have seen, however, the IMF had no leverage over the policies of nations with strong currencies or payments surplus, and no leverage over the policies of the United States under any circumstances. With the collapse of the Bretton Woods exchange-rate system, the Fund's influence waned yet further. Without an exchange-rate system to operate, the Fund took on a number of different functions in sequence: recycler of OPEC surpluses; international credit-rating agency for developing countries with debt-servicing problems; manager of capital flows to and technical assistance for formerly socialist economies. In none of these roles, though, does the Fund exercise any meaningful influence over the policies of industrialized countries, especially not over U.S., Japanese, or German/EC policies.

The G-7 consultative process, begun with the Rambouillet economic summit in 1975 and routinized if not strengthened since, has provided at least a forum for discussion of macroeconomic policies and exchange rates among the seven largest industrial countries. Over the years, the principle has been established that the participants in the G-7 process may comment on each other's policies. There have even been a few attempts at explicit policy coordination. (The best publicized of these efforts was at the Bonn summit of 1978, at which the United States agreed to decontrol domestic energy prices in return for stimulative policies by Germany and Japan.) Commitment to the idea of truly joint policymaking is lacking, though, and the G-7 process is in no sense a realistic mechanism for routine and effective policy coordination.

This is not at all to suggest that the G-7 process is without value. In a clever analogy, some observers have compared the G-7 process to a municipal firehouse. Most of the time, the firemen sit around apparently doing nothing much. When an occasional crisis arises, however, they are familiar with each other, know where the necessary equipment is stored and how to work it, and understand who can perform what tasks. Routine exercises also serve to establish lines of authority and collective discipline that will be essential in a crisis. Similarly, through the usually inconsequential G-7 meetings, heads of governments, finance ministers, and central-bank governors develop a degree of familiarity and comfort with each other and with the institutions of each other's countries that allows cooperation on specific matters when the need arises. They also come to share some basic principles of acceptable action in times of crisis.

The G-7 process is exactly that—a process. It is not an institution. It has no capability for independent executive or analytical action. It is simply an agreement among seven industrial nations that high-level officials will gather on a regular schedule and at other times when there is a commonly perceived need to discuss economic matters. There is no commitment at this time to do anything but talk.

This kind of arrangement may be sufficient in the view of those who are content with a general consensus about an approach to macroeconomic policy. The G-7 process provides plenty of opportunity for nations to explain their policies, to comment on the policies of other nations, and generally to encourage each other in the ways of macroeconomic righteousness. To be sure, a stronger commitment to such righteousness would be desirable, but there seems no requirement for any new international economic institution, a new corps of international civil servants, or even a new set of formal international agreements to achieve this end. If and when a European central bank is established, a less cumbersome "G-3" arrangement, facilitating discussions among the United States, Japan, and the European Community might be preferred. Although other countries will not be indifferent to the policies adopted by the major industrialized countries, placing discussions among the big three economies in a forum that includes many other players (e.g., the IMF) would serve no obvious purpose and would probably merely complicate matters.

For a formal system of fixed exchange rates among the big three currencies, new, formal, and very detailed agreements would be required laying out precisely the responsibilities of individual countries in specific circumstances. Possibly, the rules of this new system would be something like those that currently govern the Exchange Rate Mechanism (ERM) of the European Monetary System. Participants in the ERM agree to maintain bilateral exchange rates within specified bands. They also agree to maintain the value of their currencies, again within specified bands, with respect to a weighted average of all the currencies in the system. (In the ERM, this weighted average is the ECU.) This latter provision makes it clear which country has a responsibility to act when a bilateral exchange rate nears the limits of allowed variation.

The experience of the ERM, though, also suggests that no new international institution or bureaucracy will necessarily be required to operate a fixed-exchange-rate system among a few major currencies. The ERM operates today—reasonably well, at least from a bureaucratic point of view—without the assistance of any international agency or staff. There is simply an agreement to abide by clearly spelled-out rules, and a commitment by national monetary authorities to consult with each other if it becomes necessary to adjust target exchange rates.

In short, whether one prefers a formal system of fixed exchange rates or simply greater dedication to a common goal of noninflationary growth, there does not appear to be a need for a new international agency or institution. What is lacking is a clear statement of the rules of the game and a political commitment to abide by these rules.

Chapter Three

INTERNATIONAL TRADE AND INVESTMENT

For most of the postwar era, international trade relations have been shaped by the principles elaborated in the General Agreement on Tariffs and Trade (GATT). These principles—market determination of trade patterns, nonintervention by governments, national treatment,[1] nondiscrimination, and multilateralism—have served the world well. International trade has expanded more rapidly than incomes, and major trade wars and significant reductions in the volume of world trade have been avoided.

Whether the GATT principles can continue to shape the trading environment in the future, whether they can provide the basis for further expansions of world trade, is now in doubt, however. The current round of multilateral trade negotiations has been stalled for nearly three years. Frustrated by their inability to remove what they see as trade barriers, governments are turning increasingly to "managed trade" arrangements, negotiating specific trade patterns rather than simply negotiating trading rules and leaving actual trade patterns to be determined by market forces. In violation of the principle of nondiscrimination, governments are also seeking to cut trade deals on a bilateral basis, without consultation with other potentially affected nations.

Ironically, the gravest threats to GATT principles may arise from the past success of the GATT process. The initial focus of the GATT pro-

---

[1]The principle of national treatment requires that products originating abroad be afforded the same treatment (with regard to, for example, taxation, safety standards, registration requirements, and so on) as domestic products.

25

cess was on reducing tariffs. Because tariff barriers are visible and easy to quantify, large groups of nations could agree on relatively simple quantitative reductions, "We all agree to reduce tariffs an average of 30 percent," for example. This made tariff reduction a natural and particularly manageable subject for large-scale, multilateral negotiations.

But the task of eliminating tariffs is nearly done. After the implementation of agreements reached during the Tokyo Round of trade negotiations (concluded in 1979), the average U.S. tariff rate on imported industrial goods was only 4.4 percent.[2] Comparable figures for the European Community and for Japan were 4.7 and 2.8 percent, respectively.

With tariffs much reduced on most industrial items, international trade negotiators must now face a bewildering multiplicity of nontariff barriers to trade. These barriers are often difficult to quantify. Sometimes they are hard even to identify. It can be difficult, for example, to distinguish between intentional barriers to trade and the trade consequences of local customs and ways of doing business. The former are clearly legitimate subjects for trade negotiations. Efforts to change the latter can touch some raw political nerves, as U.S. negotiators have learned in their dealings with Japan. Because nontariff barriers do not lend themselves to straightforward quantification, the simple across-the-board percentage reductions in restrictions that have characterized past rounds of negotiations are no longer possible.[3] The contracting parties to the GATT have reached some general agreements (particularly during the Tokyo Round of negotiations in the late 1970s) on the acceptable limits of nontariff barriers. But these are only very general first steps, and much remains to be done.

The growing importance of nontariff barriers does more than simply complicate the negotiating process. Attempts to reduce these barri-

---

[2]Congressional Budget Office, *The GATT Negotiations and U.S. Trade Policy,* June 1987, p. 31. This compares to an average U.S. tariff rate on all dutiable imports of 28 percent in 1945, before the first round of GATT-sponsored negotiations.

[3]Over the years, one of the goals of the GATT process has been to "tariffize" nontariff barriers to trade, making them visible, quantifiable, comparable to tariffs imposed by other countries, and therefore targets for reductions in successive rounds of multilateral negotiations.

ers may threaten the basic GATT principles. A large part of GATT's past success has been due to the multilateral nature of the negotiating process and to the insistence that concessions be granted on a nondiscriminatory basis. Because trade concessions were negotiated among all countries simultaneously, and because concessions extended to one country had to be extended to all contracting parties to the GATT, concessions that were asymmetric in a bilateral context could be seen as part of a larger pattern of concessions from many countries. On average, concessions made by each nation in the multilateral negotiating process could be matched by the sum of concessions made by many other nations. Bilateral symmetry was not required.[4]

But as nontariff barriers loom larger on the trade liberalization agenda, the principles of both multilateralism and nondiscrimination become harder to adhere to. Nontariff barriers are often unique to a particular country's treatment of a particular class of imports that may originate in only one or a few countries. Obtaining relief from such barriers may require very specific, bilateral negotiations. Rather than refining rules for trade in general, these negotiations typically produce special concessions that affect trade only between the parties to the negotiations. These concessions are not always extended to other countries. U.S. negotiators, for example, have long argued that the structure of the Japanese auto industry constitutes a barrier to sales in Japan by foreign auto parts makers. Whatever the truth of these allegations, it will be difficult for the Japanese government to change the structure of the Japanese auto industry. Progress on this matter, if any is to be made, will probably have to come in the form of special efforts by Japanese auto makers, encouraged by the Japanese government, to increase imports of foreign auto parts. But concessions made to U.S. auto parts makers may not extend to all other producers of auto parts. The increased prominence of product-specific nontariff barriers has led to a proliferation of bilateral trade negotiations. Such matters cannot be discussed in any other

---

[4]Some cynics have noted that the complexities of the multilateral negotiating process make it hard for any nation to calculate accurately what it is gaining and what it is losing in a round of trade negotiations. Agreement is possible, perhaps, because no one knows just what is being agreed to. If this is actually the case, it may simply be another reflection of the wisdom and political savvy of the original framers of the GATT.

way. Almost by definition, though, bilateral agreements discriminate against third countries that are not party to the negotiations.

Early rounds of GATT-sponsored negotiations wisely avoided discussions of trade in some politically sensitive basic commodities—agricultural products, steel, and textiles, most prominently. Trade policies relating to such products are intimately tied up with domestic economic and social policies, and trade negotiators are severely constrained by the realities of domestic politics. Progress in early rounds of negotiations was possible partly because some of the politically most difficult issues were avoided. With the obvious and manageable barriers to trade in most industrial goods mostly gone, though, GATT negotiators no longer have the luxury of avoiding the hard issues. (The main obstacle to progress in the current round of trade talks is the failure of the United States and the European Community to agree on a plan for reducing agricultural subsidies.) Also, as the developing nations have come to exercise greater influence in the multilateral context of GATT negotiations, they have insisted on applying the general GATT principles to the kinds of basic commodities—both agricultural and industrial—that are important in the exports of many developing countries but politically sensitive in the industrialized world.

The rise of trade in services has also complicated the application of GATT principles. Among the most fundamental of GATT principles is nonintervention by governments in trade matters. But in some service industries, government regulatory involvement is both necessary and traditionally heavy—in banking, for example, or telecommunications, or insurance. As these sorts of services become more important in world trade, application of the nonintervention principle becomes increasingly problematic. Different countries have very different regulatory philosophies and approaches, and forcing foreign service providers to adhere to local regulatory policies can create the appearance and often the reality of discrimination.

The GATT principle of national treatment can also be problematic in this context. This principle requires governments to treat foreign and domestic suppliers of goods and services equally. But strict adherence to the principle of national treatment can sometimes create marked asymmetries in the way two counties treat each other's service providers. German banks operating in the United States, for example, are subject to the same regulations as U.S. banks and are therefore proscribed from many kinds of business: underwriting securities issues, ownership of nonbanking enterprises, multistate banking, and so on. U.S. banks operating in Germany, though, are free to operate as *Universalbanken* just as German banks are. Such unequal treatment of German banks in the United States and U.S. banks in Germany can easily appear to be unfair, even though it is strictly in accordance with the principle of national treatment. To cite another example, U.S. negotiators in the Uruguay Round of trade talks recently threatened to withdraw U.S. support for measures aimed at liberalizing trade in air and maritime transport and in telecommunications. The U.S. negotiators argued that the United States has generally deregulated these industries and that foreign producers, once given access to these markets, will enjoy an opportunity to expand their operations greatly. Because many other countries continue to regulate the service industries in question very heavily, the U.S. negotiators feared that American firms given access to foreign markets will find their operations severely restricted. Rather than agree to what they perceived as a very unequal deal, U.S. negotiators preferred, they said, simply to abandon efforts to open trade in these areas.

Support for even the most fundamental of all GATT principles—that trade patterns should be determined by market forces—seems to be waning today. The attractiveness of market-determined trade rests on the view that nations have comparative advantages in the production of different goods and services, that the general welfare is served when countries produce and export those goods in the production of which they have a comparative advantage, and that market forces will in most cases bring about such patterns of trade. In recent years, an alternative view has been gaining ground: that comparative advantage is not some sort of natural endowment but rather something that can be created by astute government policies. In industries characterized by significant economies of scale, the firms or countries that first succeed in achieving efficient scale can capture world markets. "Strategic" trade polices—subsidies to promising industries, protection from foreign competition, relief from domestic antitrust restrictions, etc.—can aid the early growth of industries, helping them reach efficient scales of production, and thus may create a comparative advantage. In theory at least, the gains that accrue to a nation from capturing world market share in a particular industry can, in certain circumstances, offset the cost of government subsidies or protection, leaving the nation better off for the government's intervention.[5]

Few would argue with the theoretical proposition that cleverly designed and well-executed strategic trade policies can increase national income. There is reason to be skeptical, however, about the extent to which this theoretical possibility can be operationally exploited. How many industries are there, for example, in which scale economies are sufficiently pronounced to create an opportunity for strategic trade policy? What fraction of world trade might these industries account for? How long-lasting can we expect the gains from strategic trade policy to be? How hard will it really be for some other country to steal away international market share by clever policies of its own? Do we have any confidence that governments can recognize and support industries that have the potential to capture lucrative international markets? How long should an industry be afforded special treatment before it is expected to stand on its own? Do governments have and can they exercise effectively the policy tools necessary to encourage the growth of selected industries?

But these are largely the cautions of academics. Despite the lack of solid empirical evidence for the effectiveness of strategic trade policies, support seems to be growing in the business and political communities for activist governmental approaches to trade policy. Increasingly, governments are confronting each other over actual and alleged attempts to help their respective industries gain a larger share of world markets. The traditional GATT framework is of little help in resolving such disputes. Leaving the determination of trade patterns to market forces will not be attractive to policymakers who believe that today's market forces were largely created by yesterday's government policies. But without market forces to act as the final arbiter of who will produce what, we face the prospect of endless and costly warring among governments seeking to establish a national

---

[5]Their current vogue not withstanding, the basic ideas behind "strategic" trade policies have been around for some time. Development theorists have long recognized that protection or encouragement of "infant industries" could bring net benefits. As is often the case, old ideas have been repackaged to support current policy proposals.

presence in microelectronics, computers, aircraft, biotechnology, or whatever the latest "hot" industry happens to be.

WHERE DO WE GO FROM HERE?

For a number of reasons, then, the GATT process may be near the end of its useful life. The trade issues that the GATT was best suited to deal with have been largely resolved. The issues that remain are not well handled within the GATT framework. The character of international trade has changed. A larger share of total world trade is accounted for by trade in goods and services to which it is difficult to apply fundamental GATT principles. Finally, the perception (certainly) and the reality (possibly) of what creates comparative advantage have changed in ways that undermine the basic concept of a liberal trading regime.

For all of the GATT's creakiness, and for all the difficulties we face in adhering to GATT principles in the modern environment, it is hard to find any serious observer who does not view the continued health of GATT and its extension and improvement as the only sensible foundation for international trading relations in coming years. In particular, most observers attach considerable importance to bringing the Uruguay Round of trade talks to a successful conclusion. Even if the GATT process will not suffice to manage all trade problems in the coming years—and few think that it can—the GATT has carried us a great way toward freer trade and a fuller integration of the world economy. A failure to conclude the current round of negotiations would constitute at least a partial rejection of the basic GATT principles and could be the start of an erosion of adherence to them, with potentially disastrous consequences for all nations. A less-than-perfect agreement is almost certainly better than no agreement at all. As long as a potential agreement offers significant benefits to all parties, the reaffirmation of GATT principles that is inherent in an agreement is probably a worthwhile goal in itself, even if all participants do not get everything they may have hoped for.

The real question for policymakers is how to proceed after the current round of negotiations is completed. Again, there seems to be a general consensus that the GATT process can and should be strengthened and extended. There is widespread agreement, for example, that the GATT's role in dispute settlement should be strengthened.   In both the European Community and in the new North American free trade area, special bodies and procedures—independent of national governments—have been established to adjudicate disputed issues.   Perhaps some of the techniques and approaches embodied in these agreements could be adapted to shore up the generally ineffective GATT dispute-settlement process.

Precisely because the GATT provides such a valuable foundation for international trading relations, though, extensions of GATT coverage should be attempted only with some caution.   Trying to push the GATT too far risks weakening the entire structure.   Not surprisingly, opinions differ about the most promising avenues for extending the GATT.   Some have argued, for example, that strenuous efforts to reduce agricultural subsidies or more generally to extend GATT principles to trade in agricultural products is unwise until some progress is made toward stabilizing exchange rates.   (Implicit in this argument, and sometimes quite explicit, is a criticism of the U.S. negotiating strategy in the Uruguay Round, which puts a heavy emphasis on reducing agricultural subsidies.)   The problem here is that since agricultural commodities are typically indistinguishable on the basis of their origins (i.e., wheat is wheat, no matter where it comes from) and are traded in integrated worldwide markets, exchange-rate changes are reflected immediately in prices paid to farmers.   If, for example, the Australian dollar declines sharply against the U.S. dollar while the U.S. dollar price of wheat remains fixed, Australian farmers will receive a sharply higher local-currency price for their output.   Since most countries recognize a need to stabilize the incomes of farmers, there will inevitably be resistance to proposed agreements that would expose farmers directly to the consequences of volatile exchange-rate movements.

Similarly, there is some reluctance to pursue strenuously the application of GATT principles to trade in services or aggressively to seek adherence to a single international standard for the protection of intellectual property.   The problem is that establishment of uniform international standards in these areas will require fundamental changes in what until now have been primarily domestic policies. The predictable consequence is stubborn opposition to international agreements and a lengthy negotiating process.   Rather than postponing the benefits to be gained by applying GATT principles to these areas until all or nearly all countries are ready to subscribe, it might be more practical to relax the principle of nondiscrimination a bit to allow a kind of "conditional most-favored-nation status" for only those countries that agree to adhere to new codes for services and intellectual property. Countries that can initially accede to these new codes will immediately extend specified concessions and protections to each other. Other nations will be admitted to this circle if and when they can accede to the new codes. In essence, this would be creating a sort of "GATT-within-GATT," with more comprehensive application of basic GATT principles in the smaller group. This kind of approach would introduce some administrative headaches; all contracting parties to the GATT would not be treated equally. It might go some way, however, toward streamlining what many see as the increasingly unwieldy nature of GATT negotiations. There are precedents for such arrangements. Codes negotiated during the Tokyo Round on subsidies, government procurement, and technical standards apply only to those nations that agree in return to adhere to them in their dealings with other countries.

Also potentially problematic are increasing calls to use trade policy to encourage adherence to international standards regarding the environment and human rights. All nations have clearly legitimate interests in national policies that produce truly global consequences. Few would dispute, for example, an international interest in such matters as whaling, protection of off-shore fisheries, and emissions of ozone-depleting or greenhouse gases. (Controversy about the last of these is over whether there is really a problem, not over whether a problem—if it exists—has global consequences.) Policies that truly affect the "global commons" are properly subjects for international agreements, and while it is unlikely that trade regulations alone will be adequate to bring about the desired reductions in activities harmful to the common interest, there seems no reason why trade policies should not be enlisted in this effort. Similarly, there is probably a legitimate global interest in discouraging the worst sorts of human rights abuses—the use of forced labor, for example—and trade policy could provide some leverage in this regard. The GATT process might provide a useful forum for negotiating international measures to encourage appropriate national policies, and the GATT itself might be a useful legal vehicle for implementing such measures.

The rub here comes when pressure grows to use trade policies to enforce standards in areas where legitimate international concern is more questionable. Is it really the business of the global community if some nation allows purely local air or water pollution? Is it appropriate to demand that developing countries adopt the same standards for labor relations, worker safety and health, or child labor that are characteristic of advanced industrialized nations? It is hard not to see growing demands for trade policy action in such areas as meddling in the internal affairs of other countries or as pandering to special interests within the industrialized world. Current GATT rules allow nations to set reasonable standards to make sure that imports do not threaten the health and safety of their own citizens. There seems no good reason to use trade policy to try to force on other nations our views of what will advance the health, safety, or well-being of their citizens or workers, when the actions of other countries have no demonstrable effect on the larger international community. Indeed, if anything, the GATT should be strengthened to provide protections against such meddling.

NOT BY GATT ALONE

Despite general recognition of the importance and centrality of GATT, few observers of trade matters believe that the GATT alone will provide an adequate mechanism for managing international trade relations in the future. Among the stickiest issues for trade negotiations today are so-called structural impediments to trade. These are actual or perceived obstacles to trade that grow out of the basic structures of national economies and societies—out of the policies, practices, and customs that shape how business gets done. Because, for example, retail distribution of many goods in Japan is handled through small, independent shops, American producers allegedly have a hard time breaking into Japanese consumer markets. Rather than dealing with a few large and sophisticated national retailers, they must convince multiple small players to stock their products, a slow and expensive process.

Negotiations about impediments of this sort are inevitably negotiations about the nature of national societies and ways of life. Consequently, such negotiations are often too complex and too sensitive to be handled in the multilateral setting of GATT talks. It can also be difficult to specify exactly what might constitute an effective remedy. Typically, the circumstances that give rise to impediments are not fully under the control of governments, and in some cases the best that can be hoped for are good-faith efforts by the governments involved to do what they can to make life easier for importers. This makes structural impediments awkward subjects for formal agreements.

The best way to deal with these matters is probably through ongoing discussions among the governments concerned. The ongoing Structural Impediments Initiative talks between the U.S. and Japanese governments provide an example of this approach. It is probably unrealistic to expect talks of this sort to yield major concrete results. They remain valuable exercises, though, in political consciousness-raising and international consensus building, and probably should become a more prominent part of international trade relations.

There may also be a need for some extra-GATT forum in which the most advanced industrialized countries can negotiate limits on the scope and character of support that governments give to specific industries. The model here, perhaps, would be the arms-control negotiations of the Cold War era. The analogy may sound strange, but it is in some regards quite apt. If governments perceive (correctly or otherwise) that intervention can yield benefits, they will not stand by while other governments act to support their own growth industries. All, though, might reasonably prefer to keep such intervention to a minimum. The arms-control analogy recognizes that national circumstances are not symmetric and that what constitutes acceptable policy—from either a domestic or foreign viewpoint—may not be the same for all countries. Further, as was the case with arms control, a relatively few countries will have major stakes in the negotiations. In trade matters, these might be the United States, Japan, and the European Community. Other nations will have lesser, but still legitimate, interests that need to be recognized. Detailed technical negotiations, perhaps dealing separately with individual industries, might be carried on among the few key nations involved, with the final package being ratified by the larger community of nations.

If restrictions on government intervention cannot be negotiated, it may be necessary to agree on some sort of managed trade or market-sharing arrangements in a few industries that are important targets of government industrial or strategic trade policies. Such arrangements are far from ideal, but they may be preferable to escalating trade conflicts, which have the potential to spill over into the political or diplomatic realms.

Another major gap in international agreements that has become apparent in recent years is in the area of international competition or antitrust policy. As markets have become international, so have production and business arrangements. As a consequence, traditionally domestic concerns about cartels and monopolies have taken on international dimensions. Initially, increasing world trade allowed national authorities to take a more relaxed view of increased competition among domestic producers. In some industries, even a single domestic producer could be kept in check by international competition. We are beginning, though, to see potentially anticompetitive cooperative efforts among the dominant players in a number of national markets. When, for example, major producers in the United States, Japan, and Germany announce plans for a cooperative effort to develop the next generation of dynamic random access memory (DRAM) chips, we should probably stop to consider the consequences of such alliances.

It is unrealistic to expect any purely national authority to move effectively against international cartelization. Action by U.S. authorities, for example, to prohibit participation by U.S. firms in an international consortium developing advanced computer chips would probably not prevent the establishment of an international cartel. Foreign firms would likely go ahead without them, and the excluded U.S. firms would be deprived of whatever technology the consortium might develop. If this disadvantage eventually drove U.S. firms out of the business of making chips, American consumers of chips would still end up at the mercy of an international cartel, now operating completely beyond the reach of U.S. authorities.

Recognizing the potential dangers in international cartels and the impracticality of combating them through national regulation, the European Community has established a communitywide and very aggressive Office of Competition Policy. There is growing recognition that something similar may be required at a broader international level. Where to house such a function is not clear, though.

Devising and enforcing competition policy is quite foreign to the traditions and apparent competence of the current GATT secretariat. Further, although all nations have an interest in preventing cartelization of key industries, the large and diverse membership of the GATT may make arriving at any workable agreements on competition policy impossible. Members of GATT, after all, already participate in a number of international arrangements—commodity agreements and the like—explicitly aimed at exercising cartel power. Perhaps the best that can be hoped for in the near term might be an agreement among the industrialized countries (negotiated, perhaps, through the OECD) to adopt a common stance on international competition in the manufacturing sector. Even this will not come easily, though, because national attitudes regarding what constitutes anticompetitive activities vary widely among OECD countries.

REGIONAL TRADING ARRANGEMENTS

Perhaps the most difficult trade policy question today is whether to pursue or to allow the formation or expansion of regional free trade areas and other preferential trade arrangements. This is not a matter of purely hypothetical interest; decisions will have to be made in the near future. Already a number of additional countries are seeking membership in the European Community. At least one other Western Hemisphere country, Chile, has made known its desire to join the North American free trade arrangement. President Bush has proposed seeking bilateral free trade arrangements with countries all over the world. There is talk of forming some sort of an East Asian trade area. How should policymakers view these various initiatives and suggestions?

The two principal free trade arrangements that exist today—the single European market and the newly created North American free trade area—were created as much for political as for economic reasons. The political ends served by each of these—European integration in the one case and validation of Mexico's recent turn toward open and market-oriented economic policies in the other—are probably sufficiently important to justify the arrangements even in the face of purely economic objections. In the future, there will doubtless arise other cases in which political benefits outweigh any potential economic disadvantages. An example might be a free trade agreement among the republics that used to constitute the Soviet Union.

That important political benefits can arise from some free trade arrangements is not at issue. Arguably, the entire world stands to gain as a consequence of European or Mexican economic or political stability. But politically justifiable preferential trading arrangements will presumably be rare. The difficult policy question for today is whether it is wise or desirable—from the viewpoint of the nations directly involved and from the viewpoint of other, excluded nations—to create additional preferential trading arrangements or to extend existing arrangements to additional countries when there is no compelling political end to be served.

Whether one finds the prospect of more or expanded preferential trading arrangements attractive or not depends critically on what one believes about the likely attitudes of members of such a trading bloc toward trade with nonmembers of the bloc. To proponents of preferential trading arrangements, their principal advantage lies in the fact that they will typically have few enough participants to allow discussion and resolution of thorny bilateral and product-specific disputes. To the extent that parties to such agreements share common views on trade matters and have some political commitment to the success of the arrangement, it may be possible to establish effective instruments for adjudicating disputes and enforcing rulings. The European Community is making good progress in this direction, and special dispute-settlement mechanisms are a part of the North American free trade arrangement.

Because preferential trade arrangements are by their nature exclusive, concessions granted to other members of the bloc do not have to be extended to all nations outside it. While this piecemeal approach to trade policy is certainly not ideal, it can simplify the resolution of some important issues by moving discussions out of the increasingly unwieldy structure of worldwide GATT negotiations. Rather than waiting for global agreement, like-minded nations might agree to extend trade concessions to each other, thereby gaining at least some of the benefits of more open trade. As other nations choose to accede to the rules governing these free trade arrangements, they will be welcome to join. Gradually, more and more of world trade would be conducted under free trading rules. Eventually, truly global negotiations might be conducted among major trading blocs rather than individual nations. By reducing the number of chairs at the negotiating table, negotiations might proceed more purposefully. Thus, the growth of free trade arrangements might offer a practical route toward freer worldwide trade, a promising alternative to the obviously cumbersome GATT approach.

To opponents of preferential trading arrangements, the above view of the world is dangerously naive. As they see it, the creation of political and administrative mechanisms to advance the common interests of members of a trade bloc are more likely than not to lead to actions that will restrict the imports from nonmembers. Rather than providing an indirect route to more liberal world trade for all, they argue, the creation of preferential trading blocs will provide excuses and mechanisms for erecting yet higher barriers between blocs. These opponents would urge major trading countries like the United States not to waste their political and bureaucratic energies on negotiating extensions of existing trade blocs. Chile, they suggest, should be politely but firmly told that the arrangement with Canada and Mexico constituted a special case and that the interests of both Chile and the United States will be better served if both countries work for the reduction of trade barriers through the GATT process.[6] The European Community should adopt a similarly hard-nosed attitude toward membership applications from more peripheral and less industrialized European states. U.S. efforts to create a network of bilateral preferential trade arrangements should be abandoned. And Japan and the United States should do what they can to discourage talk of forming Asian or Pacific Rim free trade areas.

If the current tendency toward the formation of regional trading blocs cannot be halted entirely, opponents of such arrangements urge that at the very least Article XXIV of the GATT should be amended. This is the article that specifically authorizes the formation of free trade areas. In order to discourage nations from cutting

---

[6]Opponents of an expanded Western Hemisphere free trade area point out that increasing free trade in the Americas will not magically eliminate large U.S. trade deficits. As a group, North and South American nations have a trade deficit with the rest of the world. Increasing trade within the Americas may be beneficial, but only trade arrangements that increase exports to or (more ominously) reduce imports from the rest of the world will bring a reduction in existing deficits.

discriminatory deals with each other covering trade in only a limited number of commodities, Article XXIV allows deviations from the nondiscrimination ideal only when nations create true free trade areas in which restrictions on all kinds of trade are removed. Opponents of preferential trading arrangements argue that this article should be strengthened to specify that after the formation of a free trade area, common barriers against imports from outside the area must be no higher than the lowest barriers that prevailed in any of the participating countries before the preferential trading deal was concluded.[7] It would undoubtedly be difficult to enforce the provisions of a revised Article XXIV; it is much too easy for nations intent on barring imports to create nonobvious barriers or to badger exporting countries into accepting "voluntary" restraints. The proposed revision, though, might at least establish a useful international principle for managing the external policies of preferential trading blocs.

INVESTMENT

Currently, there is no set of generally agreed-upon principles laying out what constitutes acceptable national policy with respect to foreign direct investment. Many countries restrict foreign investment in certain sectors. At the same time, many countries, in some cases the same ones that restrict foreign investment in some sectors, go to considerable lengths to attract foreign investment in other sectors, offering tax holidays, special infrastructure projects, waivers from local labor laws, etc. A few of the larger industrialized countries—most prominently the United States—have attempted on occasion to extend national jurisdiction to the foreign subsidiaries of firms headquartered in their territory. There have also been attempts by subnational jurisdictions to tax the foreign operations of firms doing business within their reach. (California's attempt to enforce a so-called unitary tax on businesses operating in the state is the clearest example.)

---

[7]Some go further, suggesting a requirement that all external trade barriers of free trade areas be eliminated over, say, ten years—effectively eliminating the preferential treatment afforded by members of the free trade area to each other.

For all its defects, GATT does prevent some of the most blatant and intrusive governmental meddling with international trade flows. It also provides a framework, however imperfect, for settling disputes over policies affecting trade. No international mechanism acts similarly to restrain government interference in investment matters. National policies regulating foreign investment are emerging as contentious issues in intergovernmental relations, and pressure is growing for the establishment of some set of international principles governing investment.

The most promising approach to establishing such principles might be simply to extend the basic GATT principles to international investment. The trade concepts of national treatment and nondiscrimination might, for example, be extended to foreign direct investment: foreign investments should be treated no differently than domestic investments, and access granted to investors from one country should be granted to investors from other countries as well. Similarly, prohibitions against government subsidies intended primarily to encourage exports might be extended to prohibit government subsidies aimed at attracting foreign direct investment. It might also be possible to arrive at some consensus on sectors where deviations from the above principles could be allowed: defense-related industries, perhaps, or fiduciary industries like banking or insurance, where the character and resources of the ultimate owner are legitimate concerns of regulatory authorities. Agreement on a few such basic principles might lay the foundation for a process that will bring about a gradual liberalization of international investment, just as the GATT has done for trade.

But even such a basic approach to establishing rules of the game for international investment is controversial. Arriving at internationally accepted principles for the treatment of foreign investment will not be easy. National attitudes about what constitutes appropriate relations between governments and enterprises vary widely. Inevitably, complaints will arise that Country A is offering a much less attractive environment for investment by firms from Country B than Country B is offering to firms headquartered in Country A. Further, in developing countries trying to build national economies and in countries trying to establish their own sovereignty, there may be suspicion regarding the activities and intentions of foreign firms. National plans for industrial development may or may not be consistent with foreign investment in particular sectors. In some countries there may be a perception (perhaps not entirely unjustified) that national interests have not been well served by foreign investment in the past. Adherence to a common set of principles governing foreign investment will sometimes require changes in fundamental national policies. That these changes may in the long run be beneficial to all concerned will not make the process of change any easier.

Those who oppose extending GATT-like principles to foreign investment argue that the game will probably not be worth the candle and that limited bureaucratic energy and political good will could be better spent in other pursuits. More important, they argue, the principal beneficiaries of more receptive policies toward foreign investment will be the countries who adopt such policies. Foreign investment will create jobs and foster the transfer of technological and managerial know-how. Wise countries will welcome foreign investment, and this view is gaining ground in many countries. Thus, there seems little reason to take on all the headaches associated with trying to make life easier for foreign investors. The current trend seems to be in the desired direction. Why not just leave well enough alone?

Chapter Four

ACCESS TO INTERNATIONAL CREDIT

Since the Bretton Woods conference, there has been a general recognition that economic development and the reconstruction of damaged economies are international public goods. Because the failure of development and reconstruction efforts can lead to social turmoil and political instability that can spill over national boundaries, all nations have an interest—beyond simple humanitarian concerns—in assisting the economic progress of the least developed and the most troubled economies. Only brief reflection on the events that might follow a failure of reform efforts in the former Soviet Union is required to reinforce this view today.

Similarly, it is widely recognized that one country's short-term liquidity problems can have consequences for other countries. In a system of fixed exchange rates (which was, of course, what was on the minds of the Bretton Woods conferees), a country that is temporarily short of foreign currencies may be unable to maintain the agreed-upon value of its currency. Alternatively, it may be tempted to restrict imports in order to conserve scarce foreign exchange. Either way, other countries suffer some of the consequences of the troubled country's problems. In today's floating-rate world, a country in a liquidity bind may be unable to service its foreign debts, thereby threatening the stability of foreign banking systems. Failure to meet some debt-servicing obligations can also result in a country's losing access to all international credit, thus disrupting trade, interrupting essential imports, and causing economic hardship and possibly civil unrest. Everybody has some stake in making sure that temporary liquidity problems do not turn into full-blown financial crises.

43

One of the keys to promoting economic reconstruction and development and to avoiding liquidity crises is assuring that countries have access to international capital and credit. A developing or transforming economy needs credit or direct investment to build the productive resources necessary for future prosperity. A country with a temporary shortage of internationally accepted currencies needs to be able to borrow these currencies until less liquid assets can be disposed of and its international accounts settled.[1]

Recognizing that private capital and credit markets of the day could not meet these needs, the Bretton Woods conferees established two international institutions to provide credit in particular circumstances.[2] The World Bank was to provide long-term credits to support economic development.[3] The IMF would stand ready to make shorter-term loans to help member nations over temporary liquidity problems.

In theory at least, international credit for these purposes could also be supplied directly by national governments, without the intermediation of the development banks or the IMF. After all, the resources deployed by the IMF and the development banks come at least indi-

---

[1] Access to foreign capital or credit is not the only or necessarily the most important requirement for successful economic development or reform. Access to export markets will in most cases allow countries to earn much larger amounts of hard currency, and thus finance much larger volumes of imports, through trade than they could manage by borrowing. International efforts to promote economic development and reform must open export opportunities in addition to providing credit and aid.

[2] There was more behind the decision to create official sources of international credit than a simple recognition that private sources would be inadequate to the job. As we noted in Section 2, there was at the time of the Bretton Woods conference a widespread distrust of private international capital flows. Such flows were considered highly volatile and thus potentially destabilizing. Part of the motivation for establishing official sources of international credit was a desire not to encourage reliance on private sources.

[3] The World Bank was established in 1945. In succeeding years, a number of regional development banks with functions similar to the World Bank's were also created: the Inter-American Development Bank (founded in 1959), the Asian Development Bank (1966), and the African Development Fund (1964). The new European Bank for Reconstruction and Development was created in 1990.

rectly from governments,[4] and national governments do in fact provide loans on a bilateral basis to other governments both to support long-term development programs and to ease short-term liquidity problems.

The supranational nature of the development banks and the Fund, however, offers advantages to both borrowers and lenders. Loans from an international institution do not carry the political baggage that is sometimes a part of bilateral lending arrangements. (This consideration is particularly relevant for development loans, which are necessarily of long maturity. Much that is of political significance can occur over a period of ten or fifteen years, and either borrower or lender may find itself uncomfortable with the relationship over the maturity of a long-term loan.) Sovereign borrowers also find it easier to accept conditions set by a technically oriented and ostensibly apolitical international body rather than by individual donor governments. Further, international organizations with established formulas for sharing financial burdens can diminish somewhat the temptation for "free riding" that is inherent in the provision of any public good. Since new loans are typically not made until all members of an international organization provide the resources required under the terms of their subscriptions, temptations to let some other country provide the necessary assistance are reduced.

Multilateral institutions can also stimulate direct private lending by acting as intermediaries between private credit markets and individual borrowing countries. The IMF, in particular, serves as a kind of international credit information and credit rating agency for sovereign borrowers. Acting on behalf of all foreign creditors, the Fund typically enjoys better access to information about a country's economy and finances than any single creditor could negotiate. An international agency can also collect information from many

---

[4]Funds available for lending by the IMF come directly from the "quotas" of "usable" or internationally accepted currencies paid in by member governments. The development banks use paid-in or callable capital subscribed by member governments as security for loans raised by the banks in private credit markets. The proceeds of these loans are then lent to developing countries. In essence, the development banks substitute their own very good credit ratings for the sometimes dubious credit ratings of developing-country governments and are thus able to channel private funds to development purposes. In the process, the development banks—and, indirectly, their national members—take on the risk that loans will not be repaid.

creditors to compile an accurate estimate of a country's overall debt burden.[5] If there is general agreement about what economic policies are appropriate to a particular country's circumstances, creditors can band together, agreeing to accept the judgments of an international assessor and withholding credit until the conditions set by this assessor are met. Lenders can thereby gain a joint power to influence policy in debtor countries that none could have individually. An international agency can also put some distance between borrowers and lenders, defusing potentially contentious issues that arise when individual foreign creditors try to impose conditions on sovereign borrowers. Debtors stand to gain, too, if the existence of an international agency provides them with a single counterparty with whom to negotiate terms of access to foreign credit.

BLURRING LINES

The original orientation of the international development banks was toward long-term, project-oriented financing. The banks would lend funds and provide technical expertise to support particular development projects—building roads, dams, or irrigation systems, for example.[6] In choosing projects to support, the banks' analytic and policy focus was primarily microeconomic. Banks were concerned with the likely performance of particular projects and with what each project might contribute to a larger economy. The structure and performance of this larger economy were usually beyond the scope of bank analyses.

---

[5]This function is today performed jointly by the Bank for International Settlements (BIS), the Organization for Economic Cooperation and Development (OECD), and the World Bank rather than by the IMF.

[6]Over the years, there has been some controversy about whether lending by the international development banks did, in fact, finance the projects that were named in bank loan documents. The question arises because money is fungible. Bank staffs devote considerable time and energy to identifying the most promising projects for bank financing. But borrowing countries themselves would probably have assigned high priorities to such promising projects and would have used their own resources (from, say, export earnings) to undertake them even if bank financing had not been available. At the margin, then, the real effect of lending by development banks for the most promising projects might be to free resources to finance other, less attractive projects, which would not have been undertaken without bank financing.

Over time, though, it became apparent that, for many purposes, project lending is simply too narrow. Otherwise attractive projects may fail if larger reforms—freeing of controlled prices, easing of trade restrictions, reforming land tenure systems, controlling inflation, etc.—are not enacted. Such reforms frequently require financial resources. Sometimes, also, governments must be encouraged, through conditions attached to lending, to undertake these broader reforms. Lending and conditions tied to a single project will not always provide the leverage necessary to encourage borrowing governments to enact wide-ranging reforms.

In the 1970s, the World Bank began to shift away from an exclusive focus on project-oriented finance by making "structural adjustment loans" and, in the 1980s, "sector adjustment loans" to finance broader policy reforms. The other international development banks have begun making similar policy-oriented loans. A growing emphasis on structural and sectoral reform inevitably forced the development banks to adopt a more macroeconomic outlook. Increasingly, they had to be concerned with how overall economic policies and conditions might be modified to foster successful development.

At the same time that the development banks were carving out a more macroeconomic role for themselves, the IMF—traditionally concerned exclusively with financing short-term macroeconomic adjustments—was becoming more like a development bank. When the Bretton Woods exchange-rate system collapsed, the Fund lost its primary mission of overseeing the operation of that system. In the years since, the Fund has taken on a variety of new functions. In the late 1970s, it was active in recycling oil revenues and financing adjustment efforts by oil-importing countries. In the 1980s, it became the focal point for efforts to manage developing-country debts—helping to negotiate reschedulings and debt restructurings, providing some interim financing from its own resources, encouraging private lenders to extend further credit, setting standards for macroeconomic policy in debtor nations, and monitoring adherence to these standards. In the 1990s, the Fund is emerging as the principal international agency assisting in the restructuring of the formerly centrally planned economies. (Cynics have seen the Fund, since the early 1970s, as an institution—or, worse, a bureaucracy—in search of a mission, not always able to recognize the jobs that really need doing and that the Fund is well suited to perform.)

For these new roles, the traditional short-term financing offered by the Fund is inadequate. Adjustment to oil-price shocks, restoring debt to manageable levels, and building market economies are tasks of many years. With each extension of the Fund's purview, the period of its required involvement and the maturities of its loans have lengthened. Also, these new roles have meant that the Fund's financial and analytic resources have become focused almost exclusively on developing and transforming economies. The Fund is no longer primarily a source of temporary liquidity for countries—industrialized as well as developing—facing short-term balance-of-payments difficulties. Instead, it has in important respects become a development agency, granting ever-longer-term credit to finance fundamental economic adjustments exclusively in developing and formerly socialist countries.

The Fund is also being drawn increasingly into questions of microeconomic policy. The current task of restructuring the formerly centrally planned economies, for example, will inevitably require decisions about what sectors or assets to privatize or to liquidate first. Questions about priorities for public investment will need to be addressed. Redistributive policies to aid those displaced by economic transformation will be required. As the Fund's lending and conditionality become longer term and more closely tied to particular sectoral adjustment strategies, its activities will take on more of the character of the structural and sectoral adjustment lending performed by the development banks. Increasingly, the Fund's client base is the same as the one traditionally served by the development banks. The lines between the functions of the two kinds of institutions are blurring.

As it becomes more difficult to distinguish clearly between the roles of the Fund and the development banks, a question naturally arises as to whether there is still a need to have two distinct institutions. Before addressing the structure of international lending institutions, though, one must face a more fundamental question: Is there any longer a need for official credit from *any* sort of multilateral agency?

THE ARGUMENT AGAINST OFFICIAL CREDIT

With the rise of large-scale private international lending, an important part of the justification for official lending vanished. Today, many developing countries can and do raise much larger volumes of credit in private markets than could ever be available to them through the IMF or the development banks. Although these private credits typically carry higher interest rates, they also come with fewer conditions on how the funds are to be used and are therefore often preferred by borrowing countries. Industrialized countries seeking to maintain fixed exchange rates (as, for example, the participants in the European Exchange Rate Mechanism) can and do routinely raise foreign currency funds through private markets.[7] For industrialized countries and for the better-off developing countries, then, the rise in private international lending has largely eliminated the gaps in the international financial structure that official lenders were originally intended to fill. What purpose, a critic might ask, do official lenders now serve?

The most resolute critics of official lending go a step further: Not only are official lenders now redundant; they can do positive harm. Because the IMF and the international development banks make credit available at interest rates lower than could be had from private capital markets, these critics argue, official credit encourages borrowing by developing and transforming economies. The 1970s, this line of argument continues, were not marked by a shortage of credit flowing to developing countries. Just the opposite was the case. Countries borrowed too much, squandered the proceeds, and postponed necessary fundamental adjustments. The existence of official lending institutions with a predisposition to provide whatever resources were necessary to maintain international financial stability (and encouraged in this regard by the governments of industrialized countries) may also have given private lenders the impression that debtors would not be allowed to default on their commitments, thus encouraging reckless lending by the private sector as well. The result was the "debt crisis" of the 1980s, the subsequent virtual drying up of credit and capital flows to much of the developing world, and a decade lost to development efforts in many countries. Critics worry that this pattern is about to be repeated in the 1990s with regard to the formerly socialist economies.

---

[7]A limited amount of short- and medium-term official financing is also available to ERM participants through special lending facilities among central banks.

Particularly in the area of project-oriented development lending, the traditional focus of activity for international development banks, there may be reasons to believe in the superiority of private creditors. Private banks should be as able as the international development banks to assemble the expertise necessary to identify, help structure, and monitor worthwhile development projects. Because private banks are not forced to maintain staffs balanced on the basis of national origin and because they can more easily pursue merit-based personnel policies, they might be expected on average to attract and to retain higher-quality staff. Neither is there any reason to believe that there are important economies of scale or scope in development-related project lending. It is hard to imagine how financing an irrigation project, say, in South Asia makes an institution better able to recognize a worthwhile road-building scheme in the Andes. On the contrary, there may be advantages in specialization, and a variety of private institutions, each following its own nose, may provide more of the support—both financial and technical—needed for development than can one or a few official institutions trying to do everything well.

Private creditors may also have a somewhat freer hand in supporting desirable development projects. While all of the national governments that subscribe capital for international development banks presumably support the overall aim of economic development, some governments may strongly oppose particular kinds of projects. U.S. resistance in recent years to funding population-control activities is a case in point. International development banks will inevitably be tied to the governments that support them, and from time to time this will limit the kinds of projects they can fund. Deals agreed to between developing-country governments and private lenders will have to pass fewer political tests.

There is also a growing suspicion that lending to the governments of developing countries may not be the most effective approach to fostering development. Increasingly, these governments are seen as part of the problem, not the solution. Rather than lending to entrenched governments that may have done much to cause existing problems, the argument goes, it is preferable to lend to private enterprises, which may then set a new, more market-oriented tone for the economy. International institutions can of course lend to private borrowers.[8] But organizations in which governments are members may have a harder time going around these governments and making loans directly to private actors than private creditors will.

Even the traditional arguments about the superiority of transnational institutions for encouraging countries to adopt sound economic policies have been turned upside down by critics of multilateral lending institutions. It has been frequently remarked in recent years that when it comes to promoting economic development or adjustment, the most painful shortages are intellectual rather than financial. There is little confidence today that any single organization is particularly adept at recognizing the components of a successful development or adjustment strategy. In these circumstances, it might be preferable to rely on a system that distributes responsibility for decisionmaking. There is no monopoly on wisdom about developmental matters, and thus perhaps there should be no monopoly on decisionmaking.

These concerns are particularly relevant with regard to the influence exerted by the IMF over which countries have access to international credit markets, official or private. A country that has once gotten into trouble servicing its external debts is generally closed out of international credit markets until it meets conditions set down by the IMF. Private bankers have a hard time explaining to their boards of directors and to national regulatory authorities why they are increasing exposure to a country that has not adopted policies that impartial technical experts at the IMF have pronounced essential for that country's economic health. Without the IMF seal of approval, neither private nor official capital is available.

But without a consensus about the preferred path to economic growth, the role of a single arbiter of macroeconomic correctness is problematic. If creditors and debtors lose faith in the arbiter, they may go their own ways, and the international agency may simply become irrelevant. Potentially much worse, creditors and debtors, fearing the consequences of breaking with conventional wisdom, could continue to accept direction from a possibly wrongheaded in-

---

[8]The U.S. government has made a particular point of demanding that a majority of loans made by the new European Bank for Reconstruction and Development go to private enterprises rather than to governments.

ternational agency, passing up opportunities for experimentation on the path to economic development or economic reconstruction. In the current environment, no one can assert with confidence that the IMF really does know best how to reform the economies of, say, the countries of the former Soviet Union. Certainly there are those who will assert that it does not. Appointing a single gatekeeper for access to international financial markets in circumstances where there is no consensus should be at least mildly disquieting.[9]

Even if we put aside questions about the wisdom of particular IMF conditions, questions remain about whether the Fund needs to have resources of its own that it can deploy to assist individual countries. To put the question another way, is it really necessary that the International Monetary Fund be a *fund?*

Some have argued that if countries are to accept the stick of Fund conditionality, then they must be enticed by the carrot of Fund resources. But those resources are in most cases a small fraction of the international capital available to countries, and arguably the real reason that countries submit to Fund conditions is that private creditors will not deal with them until the Fund announces that it is satisfied with their macroeconomic policies. If the principal function of the Fund is to serve as a certifier of macroeconomic rectitude, why does it need resources of its own?[10] The role of gatekeeper to international financial markets could be filled just as well—if we want it filled at all—by an agency that is not itself in the lending business. Proponents of this approach cite the successful operation of commercial credit-rating agencies like Moody's and Standard and Poor's. Taking this model a step further, they argue that some competition

---

[9]Another potential danger in setting up an official institution as the gatekeeper to international credit markets is that it encourages a potentially unhealthy concentration of negotiations. Private interests in a borrowing country must operate through their government, which alone has the standing to negotiate with the Fund. The Fund then provides an assessment to potential lenders. In the view of some, direct negotiations between private lenders and private borrowers would be more productive.

[10]In some final sense, the Fund's resources are not really its "own." The Fund serves essentially as a channel through which flow the resources contributed by member governments. Any losses incurred by the Fund would ultimately be made good by member governments. Thus, there seems little reason to believe that the Fund's having to put its "own" resources at risk will encourage more careful assessment of particular credits by its officials.

among international credit-rating agencies might be a healthy thing. Perhaps what international financial markets need most are multiple agencies, independent of national governments, competing to compile the best record at identifying which countries will meet their loan obligations.

To be sure, the gap in the international financial structure that the official lending institutions were supposed to fill has not been closed entirely. Some nations still do not have access to private international credit markets, and for them the international development banks and the IMF remain important sources of credit. But in these cases, perhaps it is not credit—from any source—that is required. Typically, countries are barred from private credit markets because their economies are simply not functioning. Private creditors see little prospect that loans will be repaid and therefore refuse to lend. These assessments by private creditors may be wrong, of course, but why should we expect official creditors systematically to make more accurate assessments of creditworthiness than private creditors do? If there is little prospect that debts will be serviced, what is the point of making loans in the first place? Indeed, doing so may simply postpone—and in the process compound—the difficulties the would-be borrower is already facing.

This is not to suggest that the world community is or should be indifferent to the plight of such countries. Rather, it is to suggest that the appropriate response might be simple grants, rather than loans that are at best dishonest (because no one really expects them to be repaid) and at worst damaging (because borrowers do in fact try to service them).[11] Neither is it to suggest that there is no role here for multilateral or transnational institutions. On the contrary, using multilateral institutions as a channel for grants has considerable appeal, for precisely the same reasons that these institutions are attractive channels for loans. These institutions can insist that recipient countries adopt certain policies to be eligible for grants. Providing aid collectively rather than nationally reduces the incentive for "free riding" on the part of donors. Multilateral aid need not carry the political baggage of bilateral assistance. The point here is that there

---

[11]All the major international development banks recognize this point, at least tacitly. All have vehicles for deeply concessional lending at very low interest rates and very long maturities to their poorest member countries. These "loans" are, in effect, grants.

may be little need for multilateral official *credit*. Countries for which credit is appropriate can get it today in private markets. Countries that cannot get credit in private markets will probably need grants.

Opponents of official lending, then, would generally like to see the IMF and the international development banks get out of the lending business. The IMF might continue to gather information on debtor countries and their policies and to offer guidance on macroeconomic policy matters to any country that might seek it. Perhaps it could continue to serve as a neutral agent for managing negotiations between creditors and would-be borrowers over the conditions that must be met before credit is made available, but some critics would be happy to see the Fund's current monopoly in this regard disappear. The World Bank and the other international development banks would be reoriented toward providing grants or very highly concessional loans only to nations without access to private credit markets. The banks would continue to offer technical assistance on specific development projects and on general development strategies, but they would get out of the business of making loans on near-market terms to countries that have access to private markets.

THE NEED FOR OFFICIAL LENDING

Supporters of official lending dismiss the above arguments as unrealistic. It might well be attractive to rely on private markets to meet the credit and capital needs of developing and transforming economies, but this approach is unlikely to be practical. Private international lending has increased over the last 20 years, but important gaps remain in private financial markets. Credit of long enough maturity to finance serious development or reconstruction efforts is seldom available. Few countries are able to issue long-term bonds in international markets.[12] Neither is direct investment a practical possibility for public infrastructure projects—roads, dams, schools, public

---

[12]Why this is so is not really essential for this argument, but it is interesting to speculate about the reasons. Certainly, reluctance to accept long-term bonds is in part a reflection of the perceived unreliability of policies in developing countries. It may also be partially a consequence of exchange-rate uncertainties, which discourage investors from purchasing and borrowers from issuing long-term paper denominated in anything other than their home currencies. A more stable exchange-rate regime might make financing development efforts easier.

health projects, and so on—essential to development. No foreign firm can practically provide such infrastructure and then operate it at a profit. Consequently, development and reconstruction will necessarily be dependent to a substantial degree on a series of medium-term bank loans. Because development or adjustment programs financed by the loans may take many years to complete, borrowing countries will typically not be in a position to repay the full amount of these loans when they mature. The continuation of the development effort and the repayment of the original loans will depend on borrowers' being able every few years to refinance the original debt.

But, proponents of official lending argue, banks can be fickle in their willingness to lend. They frequently exhibit herd behavior, all choosing to lend or to withhold credit at the same time. To forgo official lending, to oppose the establishment of an official arbiter of international creditworthiness, to trust instead in the independent judgments of private creditors is to trust in something that has never existed and probably never will. Both theory and experience tell us that judgments made by oligopolistic international banks will not be independent. Even if there is no official institution to tell them when to lend and when not to, they will sometimes behave as if there were. And the judgments of this invisible arbiter can be ill-informed and capricious. When banks become skittish about lending, even debtor countries with perfectly sound policies and good prospects can find themselves in a bind. This is what happened during the "debt crisis" of the 1980s. The consequences of such a credit drought will be felt well beyond the debtor countries themselves, as the experiences of the 1980s also demonstrated.

In such circumstances, some other source of international credit will be required to keep the entire system, lenders as well as borrowers, afloat. An official source of long-term credit—the international development banks—can lessen reliance on potentially unreliable medium-term bank credit and can make crises less likely. An official source of emergency short-term bridging credit—the IMF—can contain the damage caused by a crisis if and when it occurs, giving both borrowers and lenders time to assess the situation calmly, restructure existing debts, and agree on a basis for providing continuing credit.

In response to accusations that official lenders, by lowering the cost of credit, encouraged overborrowing during the 1970s, supporters of official credit argue that it was in fact the herd-like behavior of private creditors that abetted the overborrowing of that period, not below-market lending by official institutions. Credit extended by official institutions to the developing world during the 1970s accounted for only a small share of the total credit available to sovereign borrowers. Further, they argue, a comparison of the extent of private credit exposure to the developing world and the volume of resources that could credibly be deployed by official lenders should have convinced reasonable observers—and even bankers—that there was no prospect that official lenders could bail out private lenders in a widespread crisis.

To suggestions that private lenders might be expected to show better judgment than official lenders in their choices of particular projects to finance, proponents of official lending respond that the international development banks have compiled a good record of choosing development projects to support. Retrospective analyses of projects funded by these banks show rates of return well above what has been achieved by private lenders.[13]

But to argue that there is a need for institutions with the general mandate of the IMF and the development banks is not to say that the current versions of these institutions perform their respective duties as well as they might. In recent years, the World Bank has shown an admirable willingness to give outside analysts access to its records so that serious assessments of its policies can be undertaken. The IMF and the other development banks have to date been considerably less forthcoming. Increased efforts will also be required to coordinate the activities of the Fund and the development banks as their concerns and spheres of operation inevitably come to overlap.

---

[13]Opponents of official lending counter that these analyses are flawed because the official lending may not actually have funded the highly valuable projects identified in loan documents. The development banks naturally pick the most promising projects to support. But because money is fungible, these promising projects would probably have been undertaken even without loans from the development banks. The marginal projects that were really financed by development bank lending necessarily remain unidentified. It seems reasonable to assume, though, that these projects produced lower rates of return.

Progress has been made in this direction, particularly between the IMF and the World Bank, but more remains to be done. Most important of all, there is a need for new thinking about the most promising approaches to economic development and adjustment, particularly with regard to the sequencing of economic reforms and to how IMF and World Bank policies affect income distribution, environmental quality, and the attractiveness of countries to potential foreign investors. Criticisms to the effect that the IMF in particular applies the same policy prescriptions to all countries with little regard to specific circumstances are almost surely overdone. But the problems facing developing and reforming countries are many and complex, and there does not exist a convincing or coherent general theory about how to approach economic development or reform. In the face of this uncertainty, considerable flexibility, inventiveness, and experimentation will be required from the IMF and the development banks. Unfortunately, these are not characteristics usually associated with the operations of large, international bureaucracies. The task of reshaping these institutions or finding alternative approaches to promoting economic development to deal with the complexities of today's environment is only beginning.

THE SPECIAL PROBLEMS OF THE FORMER SOCIALIST ECONOMIES

The most severe test of international institutions and arrangements designed to promote economic growth and reconstruction is posed today by the problems of the formerly socialist countries. There are and will undoubtedly continue to be bitter debates over the policies that should be pursued by Western governments and existing international agencies: whether loans or a large-scale, Marshall Plan–like direct aid program will be more effective in promoting reform and political stability; the wisdom of earmarking funds for currency stabilization; the pace and sequencing of reforms; and even such basic questions as the degree to which Western aid-givers should insist on specific political reforms as a condition for economic aid. There is wide agreement, however, that international arrangements to accomplish two important tasks are currently lacking.

Restoring Intraregional Trade

The first of these functions is revivifying trade among what were the republics of the Soviet Union and among the former members of COMECON. The disintegration of the Soviet Union and of COME-CON and the inconvertibility of the ruble and other Eastern European currencies have brought trade within the region to a virtual standstill. The consequences of this collapse of trade are potentially very serious. Communist economic policies led to extreme concentration of particular industrial processes and a high degree of specialization among countries and republics. The communist production system never worked very well, but it worked at all only because raw materials, intermediate products, and final goods could flow relatively easily across republican and national borders within the old Soviet empire. No republic or country (with the possible exception of Russia) was self-sufficient in more than a few kinds of goods. The loss of traditional sources of supply for inputs and traditional markets for outputs has severely disrupted an already failing industrial structure. Factories shut down because they couldn't get needed inputs or because they had nowhere to send output. Because the quality of goods produced in the former Soviet Union and in most of Eastern Europe is not up to Western standards, there are few opportunities to sell products in the West. Without potential exports to sell for hard currency, the ability to satisfy input requirements from Western sources is limited. With neither necessary inputs nor markets for outputs, production has fallen sharply throughout the former Soviet empire.

In both the short run and the long run, it is essential to reestablish intraregional trade (although not necessarily in the old patterns). In the short run, the only realistic markets for low-quality goods are the other formerly socialist countries, which cannot afford access to superior Western goods. Also, until the vast capital stock of the old Soviet empire is replaced, many industries can make use only of inputs produced in other parts of the empire. For many purposes, Western inputs made to different standards are of limited value. In the long run, the new nations of Eastern Europe and the former Soviet Union will be natural trading partners, with varied factor endowments but common borders, considerable experience in dealing with each other, and at least within the former Soviet Union, the remnants of a common language and culture. To fail to capture the gains from intraregional trade will be to forsake an important economic advantage in a region that has very few advantages to start with.

The problem is that no existing international institution is in a position to assist directly in the reestablishment of intraregional trade. Lending or grants from the West will most likely have the effect simply of encouraging increased imports from the West and will do nothing to encourage intraregional trade. Hard-currency loans and grants may even discourage such trade. Why buy from Ukraine, Romania, or Byelarus when you can get what you want from France, Germany, or the United States? Similarly, stabilization of national currencies against the dollar or the deutsche mark may do little to enhance the practical convertibility of one Eastern European or CIS currency into another. Even if these stabilization schemes are successful (and this is far from certain), a system of intraregional payments that requires conversion of each local currency first into dollars or deutsche marks and only then into some other local currency will require large amounts of hard-currency liquidity. In a region that will be short of hard currency for many years to come, a payments system that makes such inefficient use of it will almost certainly act to restrict intraregional trade.

Western Europe faced a similar situation in the immediate aftermath of World War II. The efforts of the newly created IMF to stabilize currencies and facilitate convertibility were inadequate to overcome a severe "dollar shortage." Intraregional trade was restored only when a European Payments Union was established under the terms of the Marshall Plan. This allowed the limited stock of dollars available to the European countries to support a much larger volume of trade than would have been possible otherwise. Coupled with requirements that Marshall Plan aid be spent on goods purchased from other European countries, this payments arrangement did much to reestablish intra-European trade.

Unfortunately, there seems to be no move to adopt similar measures in Eastern Europe and the former Soviet Union. Neither is any existing international institution well suited to creating an East European payments union or promoting intraregional trade. It is ironic that one of the first victims of the disintegration of the Soviet empire was the COMECON trading arrangement. COMECON was a kind of clearing union, with net balances settled in convertible rubles. It also provided strong incentives for its members to trade with each other rather than the outside world. Now that the whole communist economic system has come crashing down, it may be necessary to reinvent something rather like COMECON, at least for a few years. The problem is that it took a powerful Soviet Union to create and maintain COMECON. When the Soviet Union weakened, COMECON collapsed. There is no international institution today with the power or the inclination to build a functional replacement.

Dealing with the Political Aspects of Economic Reform

The second missing international institution is one to deal explicitly with the political aspects of economic reform in Eastern Europe and the former Soviet Union. Politics dominates this reform process. We in the West care about the success of reform principally because we fear the political consequences of its failure. The main obstacles to reform are political, as members of old and new power elites jockey for advantage in the emerging political and social orders. The pace and scope of reform are limited by the ability of populations in the reforming countries to bear hardships and dislocations. Failures to coordinate aid policies among Western donors typically have their roots in political differences over the objectives, the means, and the conditionality of aid.

For all the dominance of politics, though, Western donors have acted to date as if the reform process were purely a technical matter that could be adequately handled by the international civil servants at the IMF, the World Bank, and the European Bank for Reconstruction and Development. Indeed, primary responsibility for shaping the Western aid package for the former Soviet Union and negotiating the terms of this aid with the recipients has been turned over to an avowedly apolitical organization, the IMF.[14]

---

[14]The officially apolitical nature of the IMF has not rendered it immune to criticism that its policies do have political content. The IMF is sometimes seen as hewing closely to conservative and excessively market-oriented ideologies and of showing insufficient concern for the distributional consequences of its policies. Whatever the accuracy of these charges, the relevant point here is that the IMF is not well suited to dealing *explicitly and openly* with political issues.

It is easy to understand the attractiveness to Western governments of turning the entire aid package over to mostly nameless and faceless technocrats. The political issues involved are extremely difficult, and there is no consensus among the donors on many important questions. No one would emerge looking good from the wrangling that would inevitably accompany a head-on attempt to meet the political challenges of aid. Much better to try to brush these matters under the technical carpet.

But ultimately, such an approach will not work. Already, officials of Russia and other republics of the former Soviet Union are reinterpreting or seeking to renegotiate matters that were supposedly already settled in talks with IMF officials. This is not dishonest or perfidious behavior on their part. They understand with painful clarity the political nature of the undertaking they are involved in, and as political circumstances change, so must the deals they agree to. They can engage in this kind of behavior because they know that ultimately it is not the IMF technocrats who will decide whether or not aid is forthcoming. Rather, it will be the political desires and requirements of the major donor countries that will determine the shape and scope of the aid offered.

The problem here is that at present there is no forum in which competing political considerations can be debated and brokered. The Western donors turned these matters over to the IMF largely because there was no other forum in which to deal with them. What might be the correct forum? The G-7 is suitably attuned to political matters, but, lacking a permanent secretariat, it is incapable of dealing with complex issues that require extensive staff work to prepare options, seek compromises, and monitor developments. The OECD has a large and capable permanent secretariat, but has not served in recent years as a forum for high-level political discussion. Also, the membership of the OECD includes a number of nations whose standing to have a say in matters of aid to Eastern Europe and the former Soviet Union is questionable. The IMF and the World Bank, as we have seen, are firmly and properly apolitical. The task of managing the reform of the former socialist economies seems to call for an international institution that simply does not exist today.[15]

---

[15]The principal reason that no such institution exists today may be that governments of the Western industrialized nations are unwilling to bear political responsibility for the possible failure of reform efforts. Much safer to turn matters over to international technocrats.

Chapter Five

INTERNATIONAL REGULATION

Among the most striking economic developments of the postwar era has been the increasingly international nature of economic activity. Once, it made sense to think of economic processes—the manufacture of a particular item, for example, the research that made it possible, the associated financing, its ultimate sale, and so on—as taking place mostly within the boundaries of a single country. Similarly, the consequences of an item's manufacture and sale were also largely confined to a single country. Most economic activity could be effectively controlled by national authorities. Managing the international economy consisted mainly of setting rules and creating an environment that was conducive to a relatively few, arm's-length commercial and financial transactions between distinct economic actors located in different countries.

The world is of course different now. Firms straddle international boundaries, fully integrating operations located in multiple countries. They move information, products, finance, and people across borders as a matter of routine, not necessarily in response to easily observed and understood market forces but frequently as a consequence of their own internal management, treasury, and personnel circumstances. Particular functions can be and frequently are relocated when internal or external circumstances change. Even when an economic activity is confined to a single country, its consequences can often be felt in other countries, through its effects on world markets, its depletion of international resources, or the environmental damage it may cause.

That economic activities are no longer confined to single nations is not something to be regretted. Indeed, the increasingly international nature of economic activity is perhaps the clearest evidence that the international economic system devised by the Bretton Woods conferees and managed by their successors has worked well. In the years since the end of World War II, international transportation, communication, trade, investment, and finance have all flourished, with the result that truly international economic activity is now possible. What we have today is to a large extent the fulfillment of the hopes that prompted the Bretton Woods conference.

But the internationalization of economic activity poses some important new challenges for international economic institutions and arrangements. In the most general terms, these new challenges arise because it is difficult for national governments to monitor and regulate economic activity that is no longer contained within their borders. Firms with the ability to operate across national boundaries can engage in regulatory arbitrage, locating activities in jurisdictions where regulation is easiest to comply with. By spreading operations across a number of jurisdictions, firms can make it difficult for any single national regulatory authority to assemble an accurate picture of their total activities. When a firm's actions have adverse consequences beyond the borders of the countries in which it operates, governments of affected countries can find themselves powerless to demand redress. For their part, governments can be tempted to compete for investment and the associated employment by offering weak regulatory environments. The result can be a regulatory version of the competitive currency devaluations of the 1930s.

The inability of national governments to control all aspects of international or internationally mobile business is not entirely bad. Governments have a tendency to regulate economic affairs that are better left alone, and a commercial and financial environment that places some limits on government powers is in many cases to be valued. More than one reform-minded national administration has relied on the winds of international competition to blow away entrenched regulatory interests and to protect the progress made through past reforms. But some kinds of economic activity—banking is one painfully current example—must be subject to at least a degree of government oversight and regulation. If the internationalization of such businesses makes national regulation infeasible or ineffective, new mechanisms to insure a type of supranational regulation may be desirable.

A CONSENSUS ON GENERAL PRINCIPLES

Although there can be spirited debate about the wisdom or the practicality of particular types of international regulation or regulatory cooperation, there seems to be general agreement on a few basic principles that ought to serve as guides for formulating international regulatory policies.

External Consequences

The primary justification for international regulatory action is that some kinds of activities have demonstrable consequences (typically negative) that extend beyond the borders of the country in which the actions take place. Other nations will have some interest in regulating such activities, and this regulation will be an international public good. Among the kinds of activities for which international regulation is most clearly appropriate are those that impinge on the global commons: ocean fishing, whaling, release of ozone-depleting chlorofluorocarbons (CFCs) or greenhouse gases, or the use of the electromagnetic spectrum. Other activities have distinctly international if not truly global consequences and therefore are suitable targets for international regulation: littoral pollution, for example, or production of acid rain. Attempts at international regulation should be avoided when the activities to be regulated do not have obvious international consequences or when national policies in other countries can easily counteract negative consequences. It would be difficult, for example, to justify attempts to set international standards for local air or water quality as long as the consequences of pollution were restricted to the country generating it Similarly, setting international standards for product safety is unattractive in most cases. Existing international agreements allow nations to set reasonable health and safety standards for products they import, and consequently their citizens need not suffer because some other country fails to enforce such high standards.

Subsidiarity

The principle of subsidiarity[1] holds that regulation and regulatory coordination should be sought at the lowest or most local level at which they are likely to be effective. To put this principle another way, affected political jurisdictions should be left to set their own regulatory standards without interference from nonaffected parties. Global standards, for example, should not be applied to limiting pollution in a particular oceanic littoral or in a particular airshed. Better that responsibility for such regulation should be lodged with some more local regional grouping. Neither should international regulation be sought when national regulation (with the attendant opportunities for different national approaches) is likely to be adequate to the tasks at hand. In practice, adherence to the principle of subsidiarity requires international regulatory action primarily when targets can avoid national regulation by moving operations to some other country or when failure by one country to enforce certain standards can impair the ability of other countries to do so. International agreements are required, for example, on the protection of intellectual property rights because a failure by one country to enforce such rights can create a loophole that could, at least partially, render other countries' efforts ineffective.

Feasibility

International regulatory action, like similar national efforts, makes sense only when the proposed or attempted regulation is in fact feasible. This may seem an obvious point, but there are too many examples of regulatory efforts that are not and probably could never be effective: international restrictions on the manufacture, transport, or sale of illegal drugs, or restrictions on currency conversions, for example. To attempt to regulate the unregulatable serves simply to debase the concept and process of international regulatory cooperation.

---

[1]This rather awkward term is most frequently used in discussions concerning the delegation of powers within the European Community. The principle, by whatever name, is widely accepted.

The Possible Effectiveness of Informal Arrangements

Cooperative action does not always require formal agreements. Progress can often be made simply by calling attention to the actions of nations or firms that fail to comply with or enforce what are commonly, if informally, accepted standards of behavior. For example, simple identification of firms engaged in sales of technologies with potential military applications to nations or subnational groups with questionable motives is sometimes enough to stop such sales. Perhaps there should be a preference for informal or ad hoc arrangements in regulatory matters. Formal regulations, and particularly formal regulatory bodies, have a way of surviving even after they have outlived their usefulness. When in doubt, it is probably better to avoid establishing formal regulations and regulatory bodies. That way, we need not worry about how to someday get rid of them.

Four examples will serve to illustrate the application of these principles to international regulatory matters and the kinds of disagreements that can arise in attempting to apply them in specific cases.

BANKING AND FINANCIAL SERVICES

A relatively uncontroversial target for international regulation is international banking. As recent events have shown, regulatory failures in one country can inflict losses on creditors, depositors, and correspondent banks in many countries. The recent collapse of the Bank for Credit and Commerce International (BCCI) has illustrated how clever managers can structure international banking operations so as to avoid effective oversight by national authorities. Certainly, U.S. and U.K. authorities might have done more to prevent or at least reduce the scale of BCCI's frauds. But national regulation is and always will be imperfect, and failures of cooperation among national authorities make it easier for those pursuing illegitimate ends to exploit the weaknesses of national regulation. By establishing common standards for auditing asset quality and capital adequacy and through an international exchange of information by regulatory authorities, it should be possible to create a more accurate picture of an international bank's balance sheet and of the soundness of its operations. Thus, there are external consequences of unregulated banking activity, and international regulatory cooperation is likely to strengthen the hands of national regulators.

Clearly, regulation of international banking is feasible. Some "offshore" banking centers may not have the same interest in the long-term stability and credibility of the international banking structure that the major industrialized countries do, and consequently they may be tempted to attract banking business through lax regulation. But a concerted threat by the governments that oversee the world's major financial centers to forbid dealing with banks located in countries that do not come up to international standards could create a strong incentive for these countries to reform their policies. Finally, it is unlikely that informal arrangements will ever adequately detail the responsibilities of various parties in the complex world of international banking.

There is, then, a case for formal international regulatory cooperation with regard to international banking, and a strong international consensus exists on this point. To date, the principal focal point for international efforts at such regulation has been the Basle Committee on Banking Supervision. This committee, made up of representatives from the central banks of the G-10 countries, has served as the vehicle for negotiating two important international agreements. The 1975 "Principles for the Supervision of Banks' Foreign Establishments" (more commonly known as the central-bank "Concordat") delineates central-bank responsibilities for banks' foreign establishments. A 1988 agreement sets uniform standards for bank accounting and capital adequacy.

These two agreements illustrate what can be accomplished in a multilateral context. But, clearly, much more remains to be done. There are not, for example, adequate arrangements for monitoring the quality of loan portfolios held by international banks—essential if governments insure deposits or refuse to allow banks to fail. International netting operations and electronic funds transfer systems ("financial wires") handle immense flows of funds yet remain almost completely unregulated. Nor has much progress been made toward establishing international capital adequacy standards for brokerages and security firms or toward developing effective mechanisms to control money laundering. There seems to be general agreement that a good start has been made in the direction of standardizing and coordinating financial market regulation but that these matters, and others as well, still need to be addressed.

INTERNATIONAL COOPERATION AMONG TAX AUTHORITIES

A much more contentious issue is international cooperation among tax authorities. Every year, world current account statistics show a large asymmetry in payments in receipts of investment income. In 1991, reported international payments of interest and dividends exceeded reported receipts of such income by some $120 billion. It is not hard to understand why this is so. In most countries, payers of interest and dividends have an incentive to report such payments, thereby reducing their taxable incomes. Recipients, of course, have an incentive not to report, so as to avoid taxes. When such payments move across national boundaries, it is usually impossible for national tax authorities to catch tax evaders by comparing reported payments and reported receipts. Investment income can therefore be under-reported with little fear of discovery.

Some have argued that the ease with which foreign investment income can be hidden from tax authorities creates an untenable situation. The failure to tax investment income is tantamount to a failure to tax capital. Investors with sufficient sophistication and sufficiently large portfolios can move capital offshore and avoid taxes. To the extent that they succeed, tax burdens become heavier on workers and small investors. In democracies, this kind of inequity is not likely to be tolerated for long, it is argued. Inevitably, national tax authorities will have to begin cooperating, exchanging information about the identity of foreign asset owners and the income paid to them. Most governments, these proponents conclude, have an interest in maintaining their ability to collect taxes in an equitable manner. Since this aim cannot be achieved by any government individually, governments should be willing to enter into cooperative arrangements that provide for mutual pursuit of a common goal. Fair and efficient tax collection is, in the eyes of these observers, an international public good.

Opponents of tax cooperation recognize the political attractiveness of such international coordination. They argue, however, that cooperation of this sort would be dangerous, removing an important incentive for national governments to pursue prudent economic policies. The problem, as these opponents see it, is that the information that would allow national authorities to collect taxes due on foreign investment income would also make it possible for these same authorities to enforce restrictions against the export of capital. If a citizen's foreign assets, reported by cooperating foreign authorities, increased from one year to the next, he or she might be presumed to have moved funds out of the country and could then be subject to prosecution. But the possibility of capital flight is a useful discipline, which discourages national governments from imposing confiscatory taxes, allowing disintegration of local financial markets, or adopting policies that will cause rapid inflation or currency depreciation. In its early stages, capital flight may serve the function of a mine canary, warning governments that market sentiment is turning against the policies they are pursuing. In the extreme, capital flight can defeat some of the unwise policies causing it.

No one suggests that evasion of legitimately ordained taxes is to be condoned. But we must choose here, opponents argue, the lesser of two evils. More economies and societies have been ruined by foolish economic policies than by failures to collect taxes on certain kinds of income or by capital flight from wise and necessary national economic policies. Preserving the potential for capital flight should provide at least some protection against the more extreme forms of economic policy madness that sometimes afflict national governments. As we have noted before, policies in one country that support noninflationary growth can make such policies more effective in other countries, and measures that encourage wise policymaking are thus public goods.

What makes this debate interesting is the agreement by both proponents and opponents of international tax cooperation that an international public good is at stake here. They disagree, however, over the nature of that public good and are consequently led to diametrically opposed policy prescriptions.

INTERNATIONAL TRADE IN ARMS AND "DUAL-USE" TECHNOLOGIES

The end of the Cold War has not brought with it an end to the international proliferation of increasingly sophisticated and dangerous weapons. This should not be entirely surprising. The vacuum left by the collapsing Soviet empire (and also by reduced Western involvement in areas that were once contested between East and West) has created opportunities for some nations and subnational groups to seize power or territory and to settle old scores. The world remains a dangerous place, and in some regions it has become considerably more dangerous as a result of the reduction in East/West tensions.

In this dangerous world, demand for sophisticated weaponry has remained strong, not least because few nations can be sure that their potential adversaries are not also building larger arsenals of sophisticated weapons. Supply is also plentiful, because arms makers throughout the world who used to supply the Cold War adversaries are now looking for export opportunities. Few would disagree with the proposition that some limitations on the international arms trade would be beneficial. Yet to date little progress has been made in controlling this trade.

Most arms manufacturers are not multinational enterprises. In most cases, their manufacturing operations are confined to a single country. But still, national governments have a difficult time controlling the flow of their products. This is principally because there are legitimate foreign customers for many of these products, and once the products leave the direct jurisdiction of the country in which they were manufactured, their subsequent movements can be hard to trace or to control.

Equally problematic are so-called dual-use technologies: technologies and associated products that have legitimate civilian uses as well as military value. As the lines between military and civilian technology are blurred, such technologies are becoming more common. Examples can be found in electronics, computing equipment, machine tools, materials processing, and other sectors. These dual-use technologies can and are produced and utilized by multinational firms, and attempts by any one country to control the flow of products or information can create incentives for the parent firm to move affected parts of its overall operation to a more permissive environment. Faced with competition from producers in less stringently regulated countries, manufacturers of products incorporating dual-use technologies will oppose government efforts to control exports of potentially dangerous products and information. A government that does so anyway may accomplish nothing except the loss of jobs, while the products in question, sold by someone else, still end up in undesirable hands.

During the Cold War, NATO's Coordinating Committee (COCOM) did a fairly effective job of keeping militarily significant Western technologies and products out of the hands of Eastern Bloc countries. During that era, though, there was general agreement among Western nations about which other nations constituted a threat. Also, because the potential volume of East-West trade was small, the costs of maintaining export restrictions were not widely viewed as high, and it was possible to err on the side of caution when drawing up lists of restricted products. Even so, there were constant battles within COCOM over what could be sold to whom.

Today the situation is much more complex. There is little consensus any more about just who the "bad guys" are, and some of the potential "bad guys" are potentially large customers. Nor is there any longer as clearly defined a community of nations with common foreign policy interests and a sufficient monopoly on the production of potentially troublesome products and technologies to enforce restrictions on their sale. Most importantly, there is no worldwide forum in which to discuss what sorts of products should not be exported and to whom.

Some commentators have called for the negotiation of international agreements, perhaps along the lines of the Nuclear Non-Proliferation Treaty, limiting the international transfer of a wide variety of conventional weapons and weapons technologies. They see limiting the spread of sophisticated conventional weaponry as an international public good and the arms trade as an appropriate target for international regulation.

While sympathizing with the goal of limiting the spread of sophisticated weapons, others argue that international agreements of this sort are unworkable. There are few weapons technologies, they argue, that are controlled by a small enough group of countries to make joint efforts at restricting transfers plausible. As the group of nations with the technical wherewithal to employ these technologies increases, control efforts will become increasingly problematic. Regulation of all but a very small set of technologies is impractical, they argue, and the policymaking energy and political goodwill required to negotiate meaningful trade restrictions might be better used for other purposes.

One might push thinking about internationally agreed trade restrictions one step further. Recent years have seen an increased reliance on economic sanctions by the world community to discourage actions that are generally considered undesirable. Although such measures are in many regards preferable to military enforcement of international standards, they have been of dubious effectiveness. Perhaps this has been partly because economic sanctions are almost always designed and implemented in an ad hoc fashion. For years, the world has maintained elaborate command structures and secretariats to plan and support the operations of military alliances. Most of these alliances regularly engage in exercises to test their planning and their command structures in at least simulated operations. Some have suggested—but others strenuously disagree—that it is time to consider the practicality and desirability of similar command structures, secretariats, and exercises for the support of economic measures.

REGULATORY HARMONIZATION

As progress is made toward removing identifiable and quantifiable barriers to trade (such as tariffs), the remaining obstacles to expanded international trade are increasingly regulatory and cultural in nature. Foreign firms frequently run afoul of local regulations that require, for example, adherence to different product-quality standards than are applied in other markets. Local tax policies, worker safety rules, and labor laws may require businesses to structure operations differently in foreign markets than at home. Social customs and local business practices are sometimes hard for foreigners to adapt to. No matter what the origin or intent of these practices and policies, the result is that potentially beneficial trade is blocked and trade relations among nations become strained. As national economies become more intertwined—through trade, through direct investment, through the linking of their financial and commodity markets—national regulations, policies, and cultures will increasingly become matters of international interest.

Officials charged with creating a single European market have realized that truly free trade will require "harmonization" of regulatory policies, taxation, and even some social norms among the member countries of the European Community. An elaborate structure of working groups has been established to identify and eliminate differences in regulatory policies and approaches that will act to block the free movement of goods and people within Europe.

Even among countries with much less ambitious goals for economic integration, there seems to be growing concern about the ways that other nations organize and control their economic affairs. The clearest example to date of such concerns is to be found in the Structural Impediments Initiative (SII) currently under way between Japan and the United States. It is easy to be cynical about the prospects of this particular set of agreements for increasing trade between the United States and Japan. The SII talks serve at least, though, to increase awareness of differences in national regulatory approaches and business practices. They also serve to establish a precedent of governments meeting and commenting about the workings of other nations' economies. Over time, this commentary may lead to changes that will ease tensions.

Efforts to negotiate common approaches to regulation are not without dangers, however. There is no reason, opponents argue, that we should seek to make others like ourselves. If two countries see mutual advantage in adjusting their rules to simplify the movement of goods, people, or investment between them, fine. But to expend political or diplomatic capital to encourage another nation to change its internal rules or policies is probably unwise. It is, after all, differences in national circumstances that give rise to the gains from international trade. Although policies and practices in foreign countries may act as barriers to sales by some U.S. producers, these same policies and practices may allow lower-cost production abroad of some goods, and U.S. consumers could be the beneficiaries. To campaign aggressively for harmonization might serve the interests of U.S. producers only at the expense of U.S. consumers. Nations, no less than businesses, perform better when faced with competition, and the best proof that certain national policies are misguided is often the example of other countries where things are done differently.

Nonetheless, it may be worthwhile to explore the possibilities, both formally and informally, for international harmonization that can prove beneficial to all parties involved. In the past, the OECD has provided a forum for the discussion of such issues. In view of the growing difficulties in reaching international agreements through traditional channels on, for example, trade and environmental matters, it might be worthwhile to consider strengthening mechanisms for international harmonization of regulatory policies.

Chapter Six

THEMES AND POLICY CHOICES

SOME UNDERLYING THEMES

Debates over the need for or the appropriate nature of international economic institutions and arrangements frequently take on a highly technical character. Proponents and opponents of various views argue at considerable length about the finer points of history, economic theory, political reality, and the interpretation of underlying facts. This is probably desirable and almost certainly inevitable. The international economy and international economic relations are complex, and propositions that may appear obvious at first glance may be rendered much less certain after a closer examination. Detailed and closely argued technical analyses do change attitudes and policies—sometimes outright, but more often cumulatively as the weight of evidence, analysis, and experience on one side or the other of an important question gradually becomes decisive. The summaries provided here of some current debates suggest the need for considerable amounts of further research and analysis.

But underlying these technical arguments are more fundamental differences in outlook, which strongly influence views and policy prescriptions regarding cooperative international action on economic matters. To a large extent, the differences in outlook that result in different views about the need for and the proper nature of international action are the same as those that underlie debates about the need for and the proper nature of public action at the national level. In the most fundamental terms, these are differences over the degree of confidence that can or should be placed in centralized, collective policymaking as opposed to decentralized, individualistic decisionmaking. Observers who support an activist, interventionist approach to economic policymaking by national authorities often find some attraction in similar policies at the international level. Conversely, those who think it wiser for national policymakers simply to establish some basic rules of the game and then leave the course of events largely in the hands of individual private decisionmakers will frequently espouse a similar approach to international economic questions.

All sensible observers of the international economy recognize that neither approach is attractive in its most extreme form. Markets are not perfect, and the sum of individual actions will not always produce socially desirable outcomes. Nor can national economic authorities achieve all of their legitimate economic aims through purely national policies. But national interests and circumstances do vary, and the exercise of national sovereignty can bring important benefits. International institutions cannot ever reflect the differing needs and desires of different countries, and in many economic matters countries must be left to go their own way. The smooth functioning of the international economy will almost certainly require direct intervention by supranational entities or coordinated action by national authorities on some occasions. Most decisions, though, will and should be left to national economic authorities and to private decisionmakers. Differences arise over the proper mix of international, national, and private decisionmaking.

Attitudes about collective versus individual decisionmaking and thus about appropriate roles for international economic institutions derive from more specific views about the world and the way it works. Differences in these regards run throughout the debates over specific institutions.

There are, for example, sharp differences of opinion over the level of wisdom and efficiency that may be reasonably expected of governmental and quasi-governmental actors. Bureaucrats—whether national or international—are largely immune to the discipline of the marketplace, and incompetent or perversely motivated officials and public servants will not always be swept from office. International bureaucrats are further insulated from the political discipline that national officials must typically face. On the other hand, we recognize that the intervention of a disinterested party or of someone who pursues common rather than individual interests is sometimes desirable. Whether one favors the establishment or the expansion of international economic institutions depends critically on whether one believes that the directors and staffs of such institutions can be trusted to perform their duties honestly and effectively.

Similarly, views diverge over the rationality, independence, and access to relevant information of private or purely national decisionmakers. No one understands the needs and wants of any individual better than that individual himself, but doubts are sometimes raised about an individual's ability to recognize and pursue these interests in an effective manner. The same may be said of nations. Also, the pursuit of individual or national interests can in some circumstances damage the interests of other individuals and nations. In other circumstances, effective pursuit of individual and national goals is impractical without the coordinated support of other individuals and nations. Before one is willing to trust decentralized decisionmaking—either by individuals or by nations—one must be convinced that the decentralized decisionmakers do in fact have the wherewithal to perceive and pursue their interests and that this pursuit will not harm others.

Both of these matters have become subjects of vigorous research in academic circles. Students of public choice theory and political economy seek to understand the motivations and behavior of officials and civil servants. Recent research into how information is collected and used and how expectations are formed and manifested has contributed to a better understanding of when decisions can and should be left to atomistic decisionmakers. Deep, essentially philosophical differences remain, however, over the proclivities of atomistic actors and public officials—differences that will probably never be resolved through research—and they shape attitudes about the relative attractiveness of collective versus individual decisionmaking in specific cases.

Also shaping these views are differences over what constitutes the relevant time horizon. In a famous quote, John Maynard Keynes expressed his lack of interest in theories that suggest that problems will be resolved in the long run. "In the long run," he noted, "we are all dead." For those impressed with the urgency of making things better *now*, intervention by public or international bodies is sometimes seen as preferable to reliance on the eventual equilibration that may be brought about through the action of market forces. For others, more inclined to take the long view, such intervention may serve only to delay yet further the salutary consequences of atomistic decisionmaking and action.

Finally, views differ about the kinds of challenges and shocks that will mark the international economic environment in the future. Unquestionably, some of these shocks will be better dealt with through collective action and some better through individual and national action. There is even considerable agreement over which kinds of shocks fall into each category. Differences—which shape views about what kinds of international economic institutions are necessary—arise over which kinds of shocks will pose the most pressing problems. Only time will resolve these differences.

MAJOR POLICY CHOICES

It may be useful to conclude this discussion of debates over international economic institutions and arrangements by identifying what are likely to be the principal policy decisions that will have to be made in the next few years and by trying to crystallize the fundamental differences in outlook that underlie different policy prescriptions. In each of the four main areas discussed above, there is one basic policy choice to be made.

Exchange Rates, International Payments, and Macroeconomic Coordination

The central policy question here is whether or not it would be wise to make exchange-rate stability among the world's three major currencies—dollar, yen, and deutsche mark/ECU—a primary objective for international economic policy.

Proponents of this approach fear that continued exchange-rate instability poses a severe threat to the maintenance of a liberal, market-driven international trading regime. It may well be that sound national economic policies will eventually bring about exchange-rate stability, but we may not have the luxury of waiting for this desirable result. The threat to the liberal trading regime is clear and present today, manifested in the increasing resort to quantitative trade restrictions and preferential trading arrangements. Coordinated international action is required now. Moreover, there is no guarantee that nations will pursue the kinds of policies that will lead to stable exchange rates. In this view, the kinds of economic shocks that are most likely in coming years will be generated by erratic national monetary policies, precisely the sorts of policy mistakes that the discipline of maintaining stable exchange rates would make less likely. Proponents of formal arrangements to stabilize exchange rates believe that major real-side shocks that affect countries differentially and necessitate major exchange-rate realignments will be rare in the future. (The most recent example of such a shock is German reunification, which has placed a unique burden on Germany and wrought havoc within the European Exchange Rate Mechanism.)

Opponents discount the dangers to international trade posed by floating exchange rates. They argue that the world is an uncertain place, that shocks of all sorts can come from all directions, and that it is politically naive to believe that national governments will abide by international agreements that limit their freedom of economic policy maneuver. As circumstances change, exchange rates *should* change, and no international agreement is likely to prevent a nation's going its own way when an adjusted exchange rate will serve national interests. (The recent collapse of the European Exchange Rate Mechanism will provide a strong argument for this view.) Much better, they suggest, to take the long view, to make noninflationary growth the primary target of national and international economic policy, and to let exchange rates take care of themselves.

International Trade and Investment

With regard to international trade, the principal policy choice is whether to pursue or to discourage the proliferation or the expansion of free trade arrangements. The alternative to these necessarily discriminatory trading arrangements would be for national policymakers to rededicate themselves to perfecting and extending the GATT, confirming the GATT principles of multilateralism and nondiscrimination as the cornerstones of the international trading regime.

Proponents of free trade zones see the GATT negotiating process as cumbersome and GATT principles as difficult to apply to the realities of modern trade. To postpone all progress toward increased international trade until all parties to the GATT can reach agreement on a broad agenda of reforms (if such agreement is in fact possible) is to needlessly delay achievable progress and to increase the danger that growing trade friction will undermine the trade we already enjoy. Proponents of preferential trading arrangements propose to seek trade expansion on a piecemeal basis, concluding mutually beneficial agreements with particular countries or groups of countries whenever the opportunity arises. At the core of support for this approach lies a judgment that piece-by-piece progress will cumulatively approach the ultimate objective of freer world trade as local trading arrangements expand and proliferate.

Opponents of these special trading arrangements fear that they will inevitably become exclusionary. Proliferation and expansion of special arrangements will not, therefore, approach the GATT ideal of free world trade. They will instead complete the division of the world into a number of isolated trading zones, each maintaining high barriers against imports from the others. For all its flaws, the GATT provides the only reliable path toward sustainable expansion of world trade.

Access to International Credit

There is much debate over specific policies of the International Monetary Fund and the multilateral development banks and over how to distinguish the Fund's role from that of the banks. Beneath these debates, though, a more fundamental controversy is shaping up over whether the rapid growth of private international credit and capital markets has eliminated the need for substantial official lending. Underlying this debate is a fundamental difference of views about the relative abilities of official and private lenders to recognize and fund promising development efforts.

Proponents of official lending argue that private credit and capital are not realistic possibilities for some kinds of long-term development financing needs; direct investors will never be attracted to major infrastructure projects, and few developing countries are able to float long-term bonds. Consequently, developing and reforming economies will be dependent on medium-term bank credit. But international banks are fickle in their willingness to lend. Further, they display herd-like behavior, all being too willing to lend at some times and much too reluctant to lend at others. As a result, occasional liquidity crises will threaten national development and reform efforts and international financial stability. Official lenders, less subject to wide swings in market sentiment, can bring much-needed stability to markets for development finance and can provide emergency liquidity when private lenders run for cover.

Opponents of official lending have more faith in private credit markets, arguing that a reluctance to lend reflects a judgment that the would-be borrower's policies are not sound. There is no reason to believe that assessments of a country's creditworthiness made by official institutions will be systematically more accurate than assessments made by private lenders. Thus, if official institutions lend when private ones will not, they will simply be allowing the borrower to postpone necessary policy reforms. Better, these opponents conclude, for official institutions to get out of the international lending business, restricting themselves instead to collecting, analyzing, and disseminating information about specific borrowers and specific projects, providing technical advice to developing and reforming countries, and possibly serving as a channel for grants (not loans) to countries that have no realistic access to private credit markets.

International Regulation

There is widespread agreement that international regulation of some kinds of economic activity is both desirable and practical. International banking is the most obvious target for international regulatory cooperation. There is considerably more controversy, though, over the wisdom or the practicality of international cooperation among tax authorities, international regulation of trade in arms and "dual-use" technologies, and general efforts at regulatory harmonization. Here, differences in outlook with regard to the competence and benignity of governments become critical. Those who believe that governments (or at least many governments) are generally to be trusted to act wisely to advance the interests of their citizens are typically in favor of international regulatory cooperation. This cooperation will allow these governments to pursue their laudable ends more effectively. Those who are disposed to think of governments as less than entirely reliable or benign prefer to weaken some kinds of international regulatory action because they fear that such concerted action will increase the ability of governments to pursue foolish or wrongheaded policies.

A NEW BRETTON WOODS

The international economic environment is much changed from the way it was when the original Bretton Woods conference was convened in 1944. Largely, these changes have been for the better. International trade and investment have expanded rapidly, creating wider choices for consumers and new opportunities for producers. The global economy has become more integrated, and economic activity may now proceed with much less concern for artificial (at least for economic purposes) political boundaries. Although no one would describe the current international economic environment as tranquil, for the last 45 years we have avoided the sort of global economic collapse that marked the 1930s.

To a large extent, these salutary changes came about because of the structures and the institutions that were first envisioned at Bretton Woods. But the new environment poses challenges for the management of international economic relations well beyond what were imagined by the Bretton Woods conferees. The time has come to revisit the discussions and debates that shaped the original conference. Doubtless, some components of existing international economic institutions will continue to serve us well in the 21st century. Just as clearly, though, other components are in need of major restructuring. The time has come to begin a New Bretton Woods process, in which scholars and policymakers from all over the world debate the character of international economic institutions in the next century. I hope that this summary of one week's worth of particularly well-informed and stimulating discussion provides at least a part of the basis for that debate.

RAND SUMMER INSTITUTE:
RESHAPING INTERNATIONAL ECONOMIC
INSTITUTIONS IN THE POST–COLD WAR ERA
August 3–7, 1992

PARTICIPANTS

Professor Robert Z. Aliber
University of Chicago

Mr. A. W. Clausen
BankAmerica Corp.

Professor Richard N. Cooper
Harvard University

Dr. C. Randall Henning
Institute for International
  Economics

Professor Ronald McKinnon
Stanford University

Professor Rachel McCulloch
Brandeis University

Dr. Michael M. May
Lawrence Livermore National
  Laboratory

Professor Alan Meltzer
Carnegie-Mellon University and
  American Enterprise Institute

Professor Thierry de Montbrial
Institut Francais des Relations
  Internationales

Dr. Charles Zwick

RAND PARTICIPANTS

Abraham Becker

Brent Boultinghouse—*rapporteur*

Peter Cannon—*rapporteur*

Charles Cooper

Stephen Drezner

Donald Henry

Julia Lowell

C. Richard Neu

Jonathan Pollack

James Steinberg

James Thomson

Albert Williams

Charles Wolf, Jr.